Thieves in the Temple

America under the Federal Reserve System

Andre Michael Eggelletion

MILLIGAN BOOKS   **CALIFORNIA**

Contents

This book is dedicated to my parents

*Mr. and Mrs. Josephus and
Annie Lee Eggelletion*

I love you with all my heart.

Acknowledgments

I must first publicly acknowledge the maker of heaven and earth for allowing me to have life, health, and strength. I know that in our modern society, it's rare to find intellectuals who still believe in such ethereal concepts as God, but I do. I also understand that religion is a personal matter; nevertheless I truly believe Yahweh has inspired this book, so I feel compelled to acknowledge the source of this inspiration. For those whom I've offended in illustrating the dynamics of spirit in this book, I offer my apologies.

I would like to thank and acknowledge my parents, Mr. and Mrs. Josephus and Annie Lee Eggelletion for their love and devotion. For more than 60 years their marriage has been a monumental commitment to their seven children; they continue to educate us.

I must also thank my wife Deborah for her deep love and support. My brother, Broward County Commissioner Josephus Eggelletion Jr., who has always tried to keep me on my toes, has also inspired not only me, but all those that have come to know him. From the beginning of his tenure in city government, through his 8 years in the Florida House of Representatives, to his service on the county commission, Joe has truly inspired the State of Florida.

I must also thank my sisters, Erma, Loretta, Josephine, Carolyn, and Treva. You are all great and so are your children and grandchildren.

To my cousins, especially Dennis, keep up the good work. Willie Lee and Nelson, thanks for helping Daddy.

To all the employees, associates, and clients of Eggelletion Enterprises; Jerome, Carl, Derrick, Simon, Geoffrey,

Jeanette, Rock-Bo-Tim, Yvette, Shenita, Sandra, Carla and the many others through the years, I appreciate your dedicated service and friendship.

Thanks to Oscar for the website. To Bill Armstrong and David Rich and the rest of the guys at the Armstrong Automotive Group, thanks, you're the best. To the guys at Poller and Jordan; Rick, Mike, and Bob, you're awesome—thanks. Everybody at Carrera and Associates; Nick, Steve, Brian, Lisa, and everybody else; you're all great. At the Commissioner's office; I must thank Cynthia and Gwen for their help. To everyone at P.L.I.M. Inc; Lee, Penny, Don, Davita, James, Valerie, Bobby, Michelle, Brooke, Derrick, Free, Deanna, and the rest; thank you for your fellowship.

I must also thank the Mystik Radio family; Carl and Lynda for giving me a radio show. You guys saw things in me that I had no idea were even there. I thank you for making me cultivate my gifts. I can't forget everyone else at Mystik who work so hard to make my shows, "South Florida Speaks Out" and "Behind The Headlines" a success.

Also thanks to: Jr. B., Holly D., Lisa B., Waynie B., Burke at Work, Lincoln, Lionhouse, Qenmaakes, Damon, Dawn, Fitzgerald, David, Dan, Richie Rich, Jamal, Tara, Roy, Ricky, Lisamarie, Roger DJ Kareem, Claude, Waldith, Brenda, Renford, Cie, and the great Dr. J. and the perfect combo of brains and beauty Dr. Joyce Kaufman.

To my friends and guests in national, state, and county government—thanks for speaking out.

I definitely have to thank all my listeners on "Behind the Headlines" and "South Florida Speaks Out" for keeping it locked on 1580 AM/www.wsrf.com.

To Steve Waters of the South Florida Sun Sentinel and my fellow anglers Terry, Ken, Aymon, Greg, Jerry, S.A.F.E.R. and all the guys at Holiday Park; let's keep fishing.

Last but not least, thanks to my publisher, Dr. Rosie Milligan and the staff at Milligan Books; you are the best.

About the Author

Andre Michael Eggelletion, a Florida resident and alumnus of Florida A&M University in Music and Political Science, is a successful entrepreneur and the host of the two hottest radio talk shows in South Florida— "South Florida Speaks Out" and "Behind the Headlines," on Mystik 1580 AM and live on the Internet at www.wsrf.com.

Eggelletion is the only known African-American in U.S. history to publish a book on the Federal Reserve System. With eloquence and passion, he speaks to Americans about the privately owned Fed's inherent propensity to create economic and societal instability that is cloaked by the corporate media-driven distraction of political partisanship. Eggelletion asserts and reveals how the world's social, political, economic, and even spiritual devastation is the result of maligned monetary policies.

With absolute brilliance, Eggelletion daily engages the who's who in politics, business, best selling authors of the world, and top corporate CEOs. Some of his guests have included ranking members of the U.S. Congress, such as former presidential candidates Sen. John Edwards, former Sen. Carol Mosley-Braun, and Rev. Al Sharpton, as well as top nongovernmental organization officials, such as former National Security Advisor and Trilateral Commission trustee, Dr. Zibigniew Brzezinski.

Eggelletion has published numerous papers on subjects ranging from science to religion. He is also a featured columnist in member newspapers of the Black Press of America and is rapidly becoming a red-hot commodity on the lecture circuit. Visit www.talktoandre.com.

Foreword

Andre Eggelletion's work is electric. From Chapter One of this magnificent "mind opening" masterpiece he "plugs" the *eager reader* directly into a "live conduit." The switch is thrown and immediately you find yourself traveling alongside crackling "conspiratorial currents" that run down a "warlockian hot wire" to Washington D.C. "D.C." is the metaphoric acronym for "Direct Connection"! Suddenly, ten thousand watts of light extinguish the darkness, allowing the reader to clearly see deep within the bowels of the **"privately owned"** Federal Reserve.

You will find yourself walking within Eggelletion's words down the once darkened halls of the Feds "evilarchy". Be prepared to go into the shadowy operating room of America's "Frankensteinian Financial Fraternity". This is where the "Money Monster" was created. It's frightening! Not because it's fictional, but rather because it's fact. Unlike the legendary Dr. Frankenstein, who performed his experiments and created his monsters from the dead, these modern day "Financial Frankensteins" perform their experiments and create their monsters from the living.

"Thieves In the Temple" rips the cover off "the cover-up" perpetrated by moneyed madmen who justify the mass murders of millions to make billions through the butchery and bloodshed of war. Andre puts a face on these Banksters and Government Gangsters. He chronicles the history of this *Criminal Cashist Cartel* that has repeatedly created chaos to bring about control. These are the same men who *masquerade* as "moderates" and are **sold** to the Nation's Sheeple through the money monopoly's **"Managed Media"** on the Nightly Network News.

Eggelletion reveals the evil inner core of American Illuminati itself, as he "unearths" the coffin of this criminal cabal and exhumes the body of the beast that controls U.S. monetary policy and nullifies the U.S. Congress. He exposes them like Count Dracula to the "light of day." Eggelletion paints a very vibrant, vivid picture of these "parasitic creatures," which like the vampire—live only by sucking the lifeblood of its victims. We the people of the United States of America are their prey.

Paragraph by paragraph—page after page—with *punch, with power, & pizzazz,* Eggelletion puts the *odd* and *irregular pieces* of the Federal Reserve's gigantic jigsaw puzzle together before your very eyes. Until alas, you begin to see "The Big Picture" taking shape, emerging from "out of the fog." In 1913, when the Cashists first created this "perplexing political program", it was deliberately designed to be duplicitous with double-talk, double-think, and double-cross. It was meant to be confusing, complicated, and cloudy. They never intended for the public to *solve* the political jigsaw puzzle or see the "Top of the Box." Their intention is to keep us blind, deaf, dumb, and numb, forever.

"Thieves In the Temple" makes everything crystal clear. Anyone who reads Andre Eggelletion's "revelation" here will discover this is not a "Black versus White" issue. Neither before—nor after "The Emancipation Proclamation" was the American Illuminati simply content to have a nation half slave—half free. This *"Evilarchy"* wants a nation all slave—for all time—for all people, subservient to their **Lord Lucifer.**

What makes *"Thieves in the Temple"* so important a publication amongst its competition of well-documented and eloquently written books published about "The Banksters" over the past 70 years—is its **author**. Here lies the difference! Mr. Eggelletion's powerful public personality is *extremely engaging* and *profoundly important* in *winning the war* against the Warlocks of Wall Street and Washington. This brilliant book is not just telling the story—it's "selling the story" that makes the difference. This is where the rubber meets the road. André has a healthy grip on *reason & reality* in a nation plagued with people *parroting political platitudes.*

Eggelletion is "the first Black man" in American history to pen a major work on the **privately owned** Federal Reserve. This is historic in itself, but that is *not* what makes this manuscript so unique—It is Andre's *delivery* that counts. He is confident, self-assured, and relaxed *both* as an author and one of the nation's top "Communicastors" on Talk Radio. This honorable and hard-hitting author knows how, where, and when to throw the ball in "The Big Game." When the American people are *one touchdown behind* in the final minute of "the fourth quarter," this **quarterback** has the capability to put points on the scoreboard for the win.

During the last half of the 20th Century patriots from all around the country were lost and *without* **leadership**. They looked to "old white men" to *carry the ball* into battle with "The Banksters". There were not many other options in those days. There was no Andre Michael Eggelletion on the team, waiting on the sideline to come on the field to score the winning touchdown. Only a few "professorial" types and aging authors understood the *modus operandi* of the "Cashist Cartel" that controls our currency and commerce. They understood *the agenda of the enemy*, but were mystified by the maddening monetary maze crafted to keep "our people" of all ethnicities and political persuasions in the dark, confused, and going around in circles searching for a way out.

Alas, the solution! Along comes Eggelletion on a *Godly mission*. He understands that if we are to *guide the gullible* out of their ignorance and into effective action, this has to be a **"team effort"**. If we are to achieve victory, we *all* have to take on the task of tackling the **Evilarchy** who controls America's purse strings—or perish!

Anthony J. Hilder

Free World Alliance

Introduction

There is a prevailing sense of despair among the masses today in America. Anxiety, fear, and indifference have become our daily bread—all because of current and projected economic upheavals with their strangulating tentacles choking and squeezing the hard earned wealth of the masses. In America the average person works more hours than ever before only to find their income buying less and less. In fact it takes more than ten thousand dollars today to buy what only one thousand dollars would buy in 1913. Where will it all end? Why won't America's elected leaders tell us why our purchasing power is so diluted? What is to become of our future and our children's future if we continue this way? What is sure is that we cannot afford to allow our despair to make us indifferent if we are to survive. We must become aware of how we have been manipulated and deceived. There are thieves in the temple and they're robbing us blind.

Ask the average person in America today, "what's wrong with our economy," and you are likely to hear many different answers. The answers that you might hear may come from many different perspectives, ranging from conjecture to approximation. However, it is unlikely that you will hear anyone at all, or at the most very few people, saying the Federal Reserve System is to blame for the maligned economic development of our nation. This is understandable, because quite simply, monetary policy is one of the most enigmatic and mystifying subjects in the history of our time. Nevertheless, its profound effect on the lives of every person in this country is ironically paralleled by its mystique in the minds of the unwitting and victimized public.

What the average person does not know about the directors of our monetary policy, the Federal Reserve, is the fact that there is absolutely nothing "Federal" about the Federal Reserve System, and neither does it have any "Reserves." What the architects of the "Fed," as we shall sometimes call it, never wanted you to know, is that the Fed is a privately owned banking cartel that issues our currency, establishes interest rates, and operates to make a profit for its private shareholders.

So when you tell the average person that the Fed is private, upon realizing just an inkling of the profound implications of this startling fact, invariably the first reaction of many people will be disbelief. Some may say "so what," and simply not care what this means. To those cerebrally challenged individuals I can only say "just wait, if you can't hear eventually you will feel." It is my hope that most thinking people will begin to wonder how and why we have given a privately owned bank the unimaginable power to control all money and credit in America. Upon thinking about it further they might even get angry and begin to wonder who owns it, and who gave them the right to single-handedly establish and perpetuate such an economic powerhouse? What does the Constitution of the United States have to say about it? How long has this been going on? Can we ever change this egregious compromise to our economic sovereignty?

Most Americans are simply unaware of the Federal Reserve's structure and function in our society, and sadly, most don't care. Historically, the Money Trust in America has always wanted people to think that this is a subject that's just too intellectual and esoteric to comprehend. There has been a concerted effort by monetary scientists and their cronies in government, business, the corporate class, and the academic community, to varying degrees, to keep the American people ignorant about the role of money. First of all, "Civics" is no longer taught in too many of our public schools. This is intentional. If the American people continue to retain and cultivate a healthy civic perspective and if nationalism is cultivated any further in the national psyche, then popular indifference towards the negative aspects of U. S. monetary policy and globalism could not flourish. The citizenry would not allow the free market ideology to become the central organizing dynamic behind public policy in America. The American people would resist the gradual transformation of our democracy into the globally abrasive hegemonic Plutocracy that exists today. The collective mental framework of this nation would never tolerate the demise of an internationally admired, respected, and benevolent government of, by, and for the people, truly seeking peace and fair play with its neighbors.

But public indifference towards these problems is sustained in our society because we are forgetting that a healthy sense of nationalism and economic sovereignty are vital components of our legacy to future generations. We don't understand that the loss of this perspective virtually guarantees a lesser America for our children. Our primary and secondary level academic institutions could easily include a basic element of economics within its curriculums, designed to plant the seeds of a healthy civic perspective. They could demystify money, and not only teach the individual how to become its master and not its slave, but also illustrate what a realistic and sound monetary policy should look like in our modern capitalistic society.

Recently we have all seen, by way of upheavals on Wall Street, how important a basic understanding of money and investment can be for us all. Still more Americans today than ever before are plowing their hard earned savings into the Stock Market without truly understanding the volatile dynamics of Wall Street. We simply give our money to brokers and pray. As a result of our collective ignorance, Americans lost 60% of their investments in the period of corporate scandals that rocked America in the beginning of this decade. This did not have to happen. If we understood how it had happened before in America between 1929 and 1939, we would have been able to read the signs, and take evasive action to protect and insulate ourselves.

Professor Carroll Quigley's classic book, *"Tragedy and Hope,"* points out how money and its issuance has historically been used to control the rate, pace, and sequence of the development of modern civilization. But under the helter skelter contemporary climate of borderless trade, capitalization, and investment, not only has power shifted away from governments to corporations and central bankers, but now even central bankers themselves are struggling to control and maintain stability within today's globalized capital and financial markets.

The most cherished asset of monetary scientists and central bankers in their struggle to manage the changing world economy over the last 50 years has been their anonymity. In their eyes, their anonymous presence has become indispensable in dealing with the unparalleled chaos of a world without economic borders and daily fluctuating currency values. They believe that it is only the invisible stewardship of central bankers, and not the highly visible hand of governments attempting to guide our economic destiny, that is most vital in maintaining public confidence in the system. As renowned author and former staff reporter for "Forbes Magazine," Steven Solomon said in his book, *"The Confidence Game,"* which is a riveting account of how un-elected central bankers are frantically trying to govern the changing and volatile world economy: *"When economies were growing smoothly, central bankers were nearly invisible. This was as they preferred: not because they were men of shrinking egos, but because the delicacy of their anomalous political positions and the source of their influence with financial markets demanded it ... with economic fates more tied to the unpredictable course of violate financial market expectations, central bankers increasingly felt reliant on maintaining confidence-with diminishing tangible power to back it up if and when they were challenged."*

It is my contention that democracy without reasonable transparency, especially with regard to our money and its issuance, is no democracy at all. The founding fathers, though morally bankrupt because of their policy positions towards slavery and manifest destiny, were wise enough to have learned from their experiences in the old world, just how oppressive a maligned money policy can be. They, therefore, throughout the history of the epic battle between political and monetary scientists over money and its issuance, constitution-ally outlawed the private control of money and credit. Unfortunately, that changed once again in 1913 with the establishment of our fourth failed experiment with a privately owned central bank. I say that if matters of national economics are determined to be aspects of our government's physiology, then there should be in existence an appropriate regulatory structure within the government's anatomy, wherein only we the people can control it.

America's reckless acquisition of debt has been the result of spineless politicians who are either unable or un-willing to curb spending. They have put America in the same need for financial assistance as many working class individ-uals, who today must turn to companies specializing in debt consolidation into the proverbial "one low monthly payment" with its high interest, to save their necks.

It is my hope that this book will not only demystify the economic forces that have tossed mankind to and fro through-out history, but that it will ignite enough indignation within the consciousness of the American people, that we will begin to acknowledge a greater need for solidarity within the working class, without distinction of race, religion, gender, or any other factor of distraction. For far too long racism has been used by the ruling class elite as a smoke screen, cloaking one of the most draconian forces upon the lives of all Americans: debt slavery. Until we can wake up from our deep sleep of ignorance and indifference, as well as racial, class, and ideological prejudice, and begin to unite with a basic common understanding of our predicament, there will be little hope that government of the people, by the people, and for the people shall not perish from the earth. We claim to be a God fearing nation but we have forgotten that the Bible said: *"The rich ruleth over the poor, and the borrower is servant to the lender."* If this is true, and I believe that it is, then we had better wake up, because what we all share in America, regardless of our race, creed, or sex, can be only described as economic slavery in the 21st century.

Chapter One

What is the Federal Reserve?

*T*he name "Federal Reserve" is deceptive, because the institution is not Federal and neither are there any Reserves. The Federal Reserve is a privately owned corporation. It's a banking cartel that is set up for profit. The Federal Reserve, America's fourth privately owned central bank, was granted the unconstitutional privilege by Congress in 1913, to coin and print money (Federal Reserve Notes) and set interest rates for the U.S. economy. The Constitution of the United States strictly prohibits any institution, except Congress, from issuing our money in America. It specifically states in Article 1 – Section 8 – Paragraph 5 that Congress alone shall reserve the right: *"To coin money, regulate the value thereof, and of foreign coins, and the standard of weights and measures."* In other words, our coins are supposed to contain a specific and just amount of precious metal. But just take a look at our coins today and you'll have to agree that there is no silver in them anymore. What happened to the silver? Why has our wealth been replaced with worthless slugs?

There have been many brave elected officials who have warned the American people at great peril to themselves about what exactly the Federal Reserve System is, what it does, and what it means to us all. One of them was Congressman Wright Patman, Chairman of the House Banking and Currency Committee during the Roosevelt years. Patman confirmed the fact that the Federal Reserve is private when he said: *"In the United States today we have in effect two governments. We have the duly constituted government. Then we have an independent, uncontrolled and uncoordinated government in the Federal Reserve System, operating the money powers which are reserved to Congress by the constitution."*

Another brave elected official, Rep. Ron Paul, has even stood on the floor of the U.S. House of Representatives, September 10, 2002, and introduced a bill to abolish the Federal Reserve System. I shall include his remarks here in their entirety: *"Mr. Speaker, I rise to introduce legislation to restore financial stability to America's economy by abolishing the Federal Reserve. I also ask unanimous consent to insert the attached article by Lew Rockwell, president of the Ludwig Von Mises Institute, which explains the benefit of abolishing the Fed, and restoring the gold standard, into record. Since the creation of the Federal Reserve, middle and working-class Americans have been victimized by a boom-and-bust monetary policy. In addition, most Americans have suffered a steadily eroding purchasing power because of the Federal Reserve's inflationary policies. This represents a real, if hidden, tax imposed on the American people.*

"From the great depression to the stagflation of the seventies, to the burst of the dotcom bubble last year, every economic downturn suffered by the country over the last 80

years can be traced to Federal Reserve policy. The Fed has followed a consistent policy of flooding the economy with easy money, leading to a misallocation of resources and an artificial "boom" followed by a recession or depression when the Fed-created bubble bursts.

"With a stable currency, American exporters will no longer be held hostage to an erratic monetary policy. Stabilizing the currency will also give Americans new incentives to save as they will no longer have to fear inflation eroding their savings. Those members concerned about increasing America's exports or the low rate of savings should be enthusiastic supporters of this legislation.

"Though the Federal Reserve policy harms the average American, it benefits those in a position to take advantage of the cycles in monetary policy. The main beneficiaries are those who receive access to artificially inflated money and/or credit before the inflationary effects of the policy impact the entire economy. Federal Reserve policies also benefit big spending politicians who use inflated currency created by the Fed to hide the true costs of the welfare-warfare state. It is time for Congress to put the interests of the American people ahead of the special interests and their own appetite for big government.

"Abolishing the Federal Reserve will allow Congress to restart its Constitutional authority over monetary policy. The United States Constitution grants to Congress the authority to coin money and regulate the value of the currency. The Constitution does not give Congress the authority to delegate control over monetary policy to a central bank. Furthermore, the Constitution certainly does not empower the federal government to erode the American standard of living via an inflationary monetary policy.

"In fact, Congress' constitutional mandate regarding monetary policy should only permit currency backed by stable

commodities such as silver and gold to be used as legal tender. Therefore, abolishing the Federal Reserve and returning to a constitutional system will enable America to return to the type of monetary system envisioned by our nation's founders: one where the value of money is consistent because it is tied to a commodity such as gold. Such a monetary system is the basis of a true free-market economy.

"In conclusion, Mr. Speaker, I urge my colleagues to stand up for working Americans by putting an end to the manipulation of the money supply which erodes Americans' standard of living, enlarges big government, and enriches well-connected elites, by cosponsoring my legislation to abolish the Federal Reserve." Although I disagree with the Representative on a return to the gold standard as a solution, largely because of the long history of failure in such policy, which I shall discuss later in this book (see the section on the Revolutionary War), I do agree that the Federal Reserve should be abolished. I also concur with his summary of the erosion of the purchasing power of our currency being the direct consequence of the Feds' inflationary policies. I also agree with the Representative on inflation being a hidden tax.

Unfortunately for the American people, survival is becoming more difficult in today's economic climate. Whereas in 1913, a single income could provide all of the basic needs for the family—food, clothing, shelter, health care, education, and even a small amount left over for savings, today, it takes two, or for some, three incomes, to barely make the ends meet. Nevertheless, we must understand the hidden but true nature and origin of our economic problems. But people are so busy just trying to earn a living that they don't have time to read a newspaper, read a book, or watch the news on TV. If we don't find out what is the problem on our own, we may never know.

The corporate-and banking-controlled media and the government won't tell us, and unless we find out, we will remain victims of these elitist inspired institutions and their systematic exploitation of our collective ignorance. As our standard of living, which used to provide time to cultivate a healthy political perspective, continues to evaporate, the chances that a majority of Americans will ever enjoy the historical kind of prosperity that America is capable of offering, becomes increasingly unlikely.

Invariably, some people will never want to acknowledge the existence of a shadow government, or its associated institutions and the harsh economic dynamics this book describes. Some refuse to believe that civilized people within the American government could possibly work towards the slow undoing of our sovereignty. Some fear ridicule and reprisals from society for publicly adopting a conspiratorial view of history no matter how compelling the evidence. Either way, they have simply chosen to ignore the type of abuse in and of this democracy, which is chronicled in this book. But then there are those who have known, within their lifetime, the harsh reality of open denial of those basic human rights that this nation has espoused in the Declaration of Independence and the Bill of Rights. Those people who have been subjected to America's history of abuse, primarily blacks, women, and Native Americans, find these assertions to be highly plausible. They welcome the light. They will tell you very quickly that they wouldn't put anything past the greed of man. They understand that too many of the golden promises America has made are false. Black men have fought and died in every war that America has been a part of, and for hundreds of years were rewarded for their efforts by being treated as second class citizens. Women are still not regarded as equals in our society. Native American leaders in the 19th century have said that: *"The white man has broken every promise that he has made to the red man except one; he promised to take our land and he took it.* " But I do not intend to imply that the black man, or any other man's economic, social, and political plight, is exclusively the result of a racial conspiracy. Indeed, the white man is a victim of the deception perpetrated on this nation as well. He spends the same amount for gasoline, food, clothes, education, health care, and all the other necessities of life as anyone else. His purchasing power is being eroded at the same rate as anyone else is because of the debt based monetary system of the Federal Reserve. But those who still don't want to believe that the money policy in America is intentionally cloaked in deception should absorb the words of Eustace Mullins. In his book called **"The Secrets of the Federal Reserve."** Mullins describes the deception of the Federal Reserve System, in appearing to be government agency, but in reality, it is a private central bank, and a privately owned central bank is, in his words: *"The dominant financial power of the country which harbors it. It is entirely privately owned, although it seeks to give the appearance of a governmental institution. It has the right to print and issue money, the traditional prerogative of monarchs. It is set up to provide financing for wars. It functions as a money monopoly having total power over the money and credit of the people."*

I can understand how people don't want to believe that we have such an independent, enigmatic, and unaccountable system of handling the economy; but they need to know it is true. In the book *"Money Creators,"* Gertrude Coogan describes the secretive independence and power that Congress gave the Federal Reserve, saying: *"With this Act Congress gave almost unlimited power to what is in essence a trust, exempt from required audit. It is beyond public scrutiny or electoral accountability. It is exempt from all federal, state, and local taxes except real estate. The Federal Reserve does not operate as a corporation, which is at all times subject to its*

24

creator. The Fed is not controlled by Congress, but by multi-national corporations."

Yes it is true that we the people of the United States do not control our own economic destiny, because we do not control the Fed. The Fed is under the control of a handful of frantic men that preside over a monster of their own creation that they themselves cannot control. The bottom line is that no matter how it appears, governments are no longer at the economic and monetary policy helm, banks and corporations are. Our needs are no longer a priority; corporate and banking profits are.

In the days of the Messiah, in Israel, there existed a similar duality in government. Although Galilee was ruled by King Herod the Great, 37 B.C.-1 A.D., and later by his son, Herod Antipas, 1 A.D.-39 A.D., the real headship of the Jewish people at this time was the Sanhedrin Council. One of the chief duties of the Sanhedrin was in the area of money. They were known as Moneychangers. Quite simply, they cornered the market on the only legal tender used to pay the temple tithes at that time, the half shekel, and exacted as much as the market could bear for it. They also became skilled in the debauchery of money through the use of dishonest weights and measures. For example, if you bought 50 lbs. of corn from the temple, the priest would place a weight on the scale that was marked 50 lbs. but in reality the weight was often less that what it was marked. By using a 40 lb weight that is marked as a 50 lb to balance that weight in corn on the scales, the priest robbed his brother, charging him for 50 lbs of corn but only selling him 40 lbs of corn. That kind of dishonesty defiled the temple, and drew the indignation of the Messiah, prompting him for the first and only time, to use force in his ministry. Three days after the Messiah overturned their tables and drove them out of the temple, charging them with turning his Father's house into a den of thieves, he was murdered. Debate has lasted for centuries over who was responsible for the death of the

Messiah. Sadly, in that debate, the role that money played in shaping the political climate in which this controversial man lived and conducted his ministry is still misunderstood.

What is the Basic Structure of the Federal Reserve System?

Before we begin to discuss the physiology or function of the Fed, we must briefly examine its anatomy or its structure. The Federal Reserve is divided into twelve Federal Reserve Districts, with branches in Boston, New York, Philadelphia, Cleveland, Richmond, Atlanta, Chicago, St. Louis, Minneapolis, Kansas City, Dallas, and San Francisco. Twenty-five branches of these banks serve particular areas within each district. These branches do not compete with each other, they work together to cooperate with the thousands of other banks around the nation.

The Open Market Committee

There are three ways that the Fed creates money out of nothing. The first is through the Federal Open Market Committee (FOMC). The FOMC is the Federal Reserve's operation that buys U.S. government and federal agency securities on the open market. In other words, they purchase instruments of debt. The way it works is simple: the government sells bonds, which are IOUs, on the open market. The Fed buys the bonds, which adds money into circulation. The government, now in debt to the Fed, must repay the Fed with interest when the bond matures. This is why every penny that comes into circulation has a debt attached to it; it's a debt based monetary system.

The Discount Window

The second way that the Federal Reserve creates money from nothing is through the Discount Window. Another, less confusing, name for the Discount Window is the "loan window." This is a better name for that aspect of the Fed, because that's exactly what it is. When member banks run short of money in their reserves because of heavy withdrawal demand, the Fed's Discount Window loans them more money. So what's wrong with that? The problem is that our banking laws only require banks to keep a small fraction of money on hand as a reserve against withdrawals. Add to that, the fact that banks can loan out as much as ten times the amount of money in their reserve and charge interest on money that they don't have, and what you end up with is a situation wherein each time banks borrow at the Discount Window, it increases the amount of money in circulation. Because under these rules, each dollar the Fed loans to banks allows the banks to loan ten dollars, based on that one dollar in reserve. The person borrowing those ten dollars spends it into the economy. The business he spent it with then deposits that money into their bank account, which adds further to that bank's reserve, enabling the bank to create even more money out of nothing but a fraction of their true reserve. It's called "fractional reserve banking." Under the Federal Reserve System, this process can be repeated over and over again until our money supply is hyper-inflated and destroyed.

Reserve Ratio Manipulation

The third way that the Fed debases the money supply is through a process known as "reserve ratio manipulation." Banking laws allow the Fed to change the reserve ratio from 10 to 1, as was used in the "Discount Window" example, to virtually any figure—20 to 1, 40 to 1, 60 to 1—or they can eliminate the reserve requirement totally. Contemporary fractional reserve banking laws allow banks to create an unlimited amount of money. Perhaps this is why Treasury Secretary Paul O'Neill, in his book, *"The Price of Loyalty,"* reveals that

Vice-President Dick Cheney told him that *"deficits don't matter."*

But not only does the Fed have the power to monetize U.S. government debt, under the Money Control Act of 1980 it also has the power to monetize any instrument of debt, including foreign debt, in the same way.

Now the intelligent question that we should all ask ourselves is this: if the Fed can create all the money that the government needs to operate on, why is there a need for the IRS? Don't worry; we'll cover that question later in this book.

The Board of Governors

There are seven members of the Federal Reserve Board of Governors. These seven are appointed by the President of the United States, and confirmed by the Senate. They are appointed to serve a single term of 14 years in office. Once members have served a full term, they cannot be reappointed to serve again. Only a member who has been appointed to complete an unexpired term may be reappointed to serve a full term. The President of the United States designates the Chairman and Vice Chairman, and the Senate then confirms those two members for four-year terms. On Monday, May 18, 2004, President George W. Bush re-appointed Alan Greenspan to a fifth term as Fed Chairman, saying: *"Alan Greenspan has done a superb job as chairman of the Board of Governors of the Federal Reserve System and I have great continuing confidence in his economic stewardship."* For further information on the Board of Governors visit www.federalreserve.gov.

The Architects of the Federal Reserve

The Federal Reserve System is the culmination of centuries of banking practices built on usury and debauchery of currency through dishonest weights and measures. Seven men, meeting in total secrecy to establish a privately owned central bank in America, conceived it. It should be noted that these seven men represented an estimated one fourth of the total wealth of the entire world.

They were **Nelson W. Aldrich**; United States Senator, and Chairman of the National Monetary Commission. He was a business associate of J. P. Morgan, and also the father in law of former New York Governor and U.S. Vice President Nelson Aldrich Rockefeller. **Paul M. Warburg**; considered the brains behind the organization, was a Kuhn Loeb & Company partner, which made him the chief representative of the most powerful banking family the world has ever seen, the Rothschilds of England and France. He was the brother of Max Warburg, who was the head of the Warburg banking consortium in Germany and the Netherlands. **Benjamin Strong**; head of J.P. Morgan's Bankers Trust Company, a Rothschild ally, and Governor of Federal Reserve of N.Y., Strong was considered J. P. Morgan's lieutenant in New York. **Frank A. Vanderlip**; as President of National City Bank of New York, represented William Rockefeller and Kuhn, Loeb & Co. As a pretense, Vanderlip and Aldrich publicly positioned themselves against the Federal Reserve Act. This was done to reinforce the perception that it was not a wall-street bill, in hope of assuring public and congressional support. **Abraham Piatt Andrew**; at the time, was Assistant Secretary of the U.S. Treasury. **Henry P. Davison**; senior partner of the J. P. Morgan Co., Chairman of the 1910 New York fundraising committee for American Red Cross in Russia, and Chairman of the American Red Cross War Council (Note: the 1910 American Red Cross was a roundtable front secretly financing the Russian Revolution). And finally **Charles D. Norton**; as President of J. P. Morgan's First National Bank of New York, Mr. Norton rounded out the group who would become known as the Jekyll Island seven.

These seven men who conceived the plans for the Federal Reserve System were all representing the interests of a hidden circle of International Financiers. At the core of this circle was the Rothschild family in Europe, who today, it is said, controls almost half the wealth of the entire world. Mayer Amschel Rothschild once said: *"Let me control a nation's money and credit and I care not who writes its laws."* I agree, whoever controls a nation's money and credit, controls that nation. In our case, unfortunately, it is a privately owned central bank, and not we the people to whom it properly belongs.

These seven men all secretly boarded Senator Aldrich's private box car at a New Jersey train station bound for Jekyll Island, off the coast of Georgia on Nov. 10, 1910, for the purpose of secretly drafting plans for the privately owned Federal Reserve. In his book, **"The Creature from Jekyll Island,"** G. Edward Griffin described their secrecy objectives: *"The reason for secrecy was simple. Had it been known that rival factions of the banking community had joined together, the public would have been alerted to the possibility that the bankers were plotting an agreement in restraint of trade. Which is of course, exactly what they were doing. What emerged was a cartel agreement with 5 objectives: stop the growing competition from the nation's newer banks; obtain a franchise to create money out of nothing for the purpose of lending; get control of the reserves of all banks so that the more reckless ones would not be exposed to currency drains and bank runs; get the tax payer to pick up the cartel's inevitable losses; and convince Congress that the purpose was to protect the public. It was realized that the bankers would have to become partners with the politicians and that the structure of the cartel would have to be a central bank. The record shows that the Fed has failed to achieve its stated objectives. That is because those were never its true goals."*

Why Was the Federal Reserve Created?

Thus we can see that the popular view of why the Federal Reserve was created—purportedly to stabilize the American economy—is false. That should be obvious to anyone, given the advent of the destructive cycles of economic booms and busts they have presided over. Its privilege of coining and printing U.S. currency without the backing of gold or precious metal is unconstitutional, which is one of the reasons it was created—to thwart national economic sovereignty. It was also conceived for the purpose of subjecting the entire world to perpetual debt and transferring the wealth of the American people into the coffers of the shareholders of this privately owned banking cartel. By providing loans in any amount to both the U. S. Congress and private industry, for the purported intent of the stabilization of the economy, as well as propping up faltering foreign countries and businesses, the Federal Reserve System has made debtors of the world.

Just as it provides an infusion of currency into the economy by interest rate cuts, the Federal Reserve has become the chief instrument in contracting the nation's money supply by increasing interest rates. This immense economic manipulating power has created and will continue to create various levels of economic panic, recession, and depression. In other words, the Federal Reserve System is in total control of the financial climate of the United States for the purpose of its economic exploitation. Bearing witness to this charge is the fact that since the creation of the Federal Reserve System in 1913, the Fed has presided over the crashes of 1921, 1929, 1989, the Great Depression of 1929 thru 1939, recessions in 1953, 1957, 1969, 1975, 1981, Black Monday in 1987, the recent "Enron era" of corporate malfeasance and the current recession, and a crushing 1,000% inflation, destroying 90% of the dollar's purchasing power. So if we are compromising the

Constitution for the purpose of stabilizing the economy, the ultimate result of that compromise was the exact opposite of what was promised—a total destabilization of the American economy.

Peril of the Founding Fathers

Every American should understand how the founding fathers of the United States felt about privately owned central banks and why they felt that way. In our country, from the day the Constitution was drafted and adopted, those who have profited from privately owned central banks have fought, connived, coerced, bribed, and even murdered to gain control of our money and its issuance. We will discuss more on how this epic battle between political and monetary scientists has been waged all over the world for centuries in the next chapter.

Throughout the history of the United States the power to issue our money has been wrestled back and forth between Congress and various failed experiments with various privately owned central banks. The founding fathers clearly understood the inherent evils associated with privately owned central banks. They had plenty of first hand experience with unfair taxes in colonial and pre-colonial America by the British Parliament. The American colonists were being forced into servicing England's crushing debt, which was directly caused by the Bank of England—another privately owned central bank. In fact, Ben Franklin believed this was, in his words, *"the prime cause of the Revolutionary War."* Understanding the oppressive power of a privately owned central bank, Thomas Jefferson said: *"I sincerely believe that banking institutions are more dangerous to our liberties than standing armies. The issuing power should be taken from the banks and restored to the people to whom it properly belongs."* James Madison anxiously agreed with Jefferson's assessment:

"History records that the money changers have used every form of abuse, intrigue, deceit and violent means possible to maintain their control over governments by controlling money and its issuance."

The only answer to America's economic problems is to remove the issuing power of money from the hands of the Federal Reserve, which is America's fourth failed experiment with a privately owned bank, and return it to the people. This has been successfully done before by Abraham Lincoln and Andrew Jackson. Both of these Presidents understood that privately owned central banks are imposed on a nation, and constitute an uncontrollable and inflationary outside influence. In her book, **"The Rationale of Central Banking,"** Vera C. Smith (Committee For Monetary Research and Education, June 1981) writes: *"The primary definition of a central bank is a banking system in which a single bank has either a complete or residuary monopoly in the note issue. A central bank is not a natural product of banking development. It is imposed from the outside or comes into being as a result of government favors."* Eustace Mullins in his book, **"The Secrets of the Federal Reserve,"** describes how a privately owned central bank creates inflation: *"Thus a central bank attains its commanding position from its government granted monopoly of the note issue. This is the key to its power. Also, the act of establishing a central bank has a direct inflationary impact because of the fractional reserve system, which allows the creation of book entry loans and thereby, money, a number of times the actual 'money' which the bank has in its deposits or reserves."* In other words, fractional reserve banking laws allow banks to create at least ten times the amount of money that they actually have (a fraction of its reserve), out of nothing at all, then loan it out at interest. This process expands the money supply, thereby devaluing our money and creating inflation.

There have been those who have suggested that the founding fathers of this great nation were holy and righteous men who were divinely inspired as they laid the foundation for laws that would govern this country. I must say that although they clearly understood the economic perils associated with privately owned central banks, they allowed themselves to condone and participate in the slavery and murder of millions of Africans as well as the murder and dishonest dealings with Native Americans during their time. Their recompense was the very thing they feared the most. They lost control over money and its issuance and thereby lost control of America to the same European financial interests that they thought they were fleeing from in coming to the New World. This was divine retribution.

In order to understand how a privately owned central bank can create economic hardship for America, we must go back in time to see the chaotic evolution of this draconian European banking system and the fight for the control of money.

Chapter Two

The Genesis of Injustice:
The Birth of Central Banking
in the Modern World

Caesar vs. the Moneymen

*L*et us begin in Rome, in 48 BC, when Julius Caesar decided to begin to issue money from the Roman government, removing it from the hands of the monetary scientists. The money that Caesar issued was debt free, allowing him to expand the city and build the great monuments of Rome. Julius Caesar was murdered for this policy by members of his own government, acting on behalf of the greedy masters of money in Rome. They were losing great wealth by not being able to control money and its issuance and they simply would not allow any one man to stand in their way.

After Caesar's brutal assassination at the hands of his own Senators, the debt free money that benefited the people of

Rome so well, came to an end. The moneychangers, as they were called, were back in business again. Using murder and deceit to end debt free money, the bankers began slowly transferring the wealth of the working class into their private coffers. This began the period of history known as the Dark Ages as the renewal of a debt based monetary system, and the subsequent debauchery of money, brought harsh economic depression to Europe.

Fractional Reserve Banking Comes to Medieval England

By 1000 AD the Roman Empire had been destroyed through the debauchery of its money. Medieval England was beginning to emerge as the power center in Europe. It was during this time that early forms of our modern banking system began. As you will see, it began in dishonesty, and from the beginning the goal was to maintain a system of debauched paper money.

Gold has always been a medium of exchange all over the world but it was too heavy and cumbersome to be carried around, so a similar system of paper money that the Chinese were experimenting with was introduced in Europe. Known as Goldsmiths, the early bankers in Medieval England began issuing receipts (paper money) for the gold that they held for their customers in their vaults. It didn't take a long time for the greedy Goldsmiths to realize that they could simply print more of these receipts (paper money) than what they retained in gold within their vaults, loan it out at interest, and reap huge profits. This was the birth of "Fractional Reserve Banking," which is the form of banking practiced until this day. It is an inherently inflationary practice because bankers can put too much paper money into circulation, which drives its value down. Although inflationary, fractional reserve banking will work as long as money is not debauched to the point that the people lose faith in its ability to facilitate trade. When that happens, people storm the banks, demanding their money, or in the case of medieval England, their gold. When the bank cannot accommodate these panic runs on their reserves, the system collapses, or in the case of the Goldsmiths of medieval England, they hang the bankers.

The illusionary practice of the monetization of paper is no more rational than the monetization of seashells; both are dependent upon the faith of the people that these instruments have worth. Although an over-all flattering view of the Federal Reserve is written in the book, *"Secrets of the Temple,"* by William Greider, here the author does adequately describe the historical illusion of paper money's value: *"The money illusion is ancient and universal, present in every transaction, and absolutely necessary to every exchange. A buyer could not possibly offer a piece of paper in exchange for real goods— food or clothing or tool—if the seller did not also think that the paper was worth something. This shared illusion was as old as stone coins and wampum, a power universally conferred by every society in history on any object that was ever regarded as money—seashells, dogs' teeth, tobacco, whiskey, cattle, the shiny minerals called silver and gold, even paper, even numbers in an account book."*

But the society's economic peril is not exclusively based on the illusionary aspects of paper money's worth. An economy can still run fine on any monetized instrument, and has done so in many parts of the world throughout history. The economic peril of our society is rooted in the practice of fractional reserve banking, whether practiced by a privately owned central bank or the U.S. Treasury Department. Fractional reserve banking insures the ability of politicians to overspend and hide the costs. Fractional reserve banking increases the incentives and temptation for bankers to overlend.

Fractional reserve banking virtually guarantees the eventual debauchery of whatever instruments society monetizes, and insures perpetually expanding debt. This power over money and credit, in the hands of private central bankers, can be and is very dangerous to our economic health; as Greider said: *"Bankers, however, could be dangerous. They were human, after all. Left to their own impulses, they might be tempted to expand their loans and create new money infinitely—collecting more and more interest income, the main source of bank profits, until eventually the system collapsed of its own greed. They were restrained from doing this by the Federal Reserve."* The last sentence in that quote can be misleading, and indicative of the flattering tone of that book. Although our banking system was uncoordinated and very harmful in the years after the Civil War, and the nation's banks are restrained from individual greed by centralization, the Fed is doing just as much damage now that the system is under its central control as was done during the wildcat period following the Civil War. You need only take a look at the astronomical rise in debt since the creation of the Federal Reserve System to see that the Fed has been a monumental failure at curbing the over-all expansion of our national debt. When the Fed was created in 1913, the national debt was just under \$3 billion. Today our national debt is over \$7.16 trillion. The only truth to the last sentence in that quote, is the fact that the Federal Reserve remains the prime lender to the government, and as such, it alone controls the expansion of our nation's debt, not banks in general. If banks in general were the primary lenders to the government, the Fed would be there to modify their reserves as the lender of last resort.

The Struggle for the Control of Monetary Policy in Early Europe

By 1100 AD, the British Empire, under King Henry I, ruled the world. Advocating an economically sovereign monetary system, King Henry I devised a creative and highly successful means to facilitate trade, and take back the issuance of money from the Goldsmiths. Under his very creative system, currency became a simple stick of wood known as a "Tally Stick." Tally Sticks were long wooden rods that were first notched, then cut in half lengthwise, so that the matching side could be spent into the economy without the possibility of counterfeiting. The Tally Stick system lasted for centuries and built the British Empire. The Bank of England despised the system because they could not make interest on its issuance. The bankers fought it relentlessly. By the time the Bank of England was formed in 1694 they had successfully defeated the Tally Stick system.

In the 1500s King Henry VIII allowed the bankers to regain control of monetary policy, once again putting the bankers back in business. They immediately went to work, flooding England with debt-based money, until the economy was in ruins. So not only was Henry the VIII a murderer of his wives, but he was an accomplice in the murder of the economic welfare of his subjects.

Attempting to take control of England's money problems, Queen Mary overturned the policies of Henry VIII, and re-instituted fair and practical lending laws. In a retaliatory response, the bankers severely restricted the money supply until England was plunged into depression again. It wasn't until Queen Elizabeth I began issuing money from the treasury that control over the money supply was finally wrestled away from the bankers. Prosperity flourished in England once again, and lasted until the death of King Charles, and then the moneychangers took over again. This time, to insure their control of England's money supply would be sustained, they immersed England into years of war, revolution, and ulti-mately, debt. We should all understand that war is the greatest generator of debt that man has ever known. And the interest generated by England's costly wars made the private banking establishment filthy rich. They were able to then establish the City of London as the world's leading financial center.

Around 1694, the people in England once again lost faith in their government's ability to handle their economy. The British subjects were unwilling to allow the government to increase taxes or borrow. The government became desperate to raise revenue. Therefore, the political and monetary scientists formed an historic alliance, establishing the world's first privately owned central bank; The Bank of England. G. Edward Griffin, in *"The Creature from Jekyll Island,"* tells us that secret meetings between the British government and the banking establishment were held in Mercer's Chapel in London. There they came up with a seven-point plan serving their mutual agenda.

1. *The government would allow the monetary scientists to form a bank.*
2. *The bank would issue fractional bank notes (paper currency).*
3. *Only a small portion of the money created out of nothing would be backed by gold.*
4. *The bank would finance government requests through loans.*
5. *The government would guarantee loans these received with bonds.*
6. *The government would then pay approximately 8% interest on paper bank notes which were only partially backed by gold.*
7. *Then the bank could use the government bonds as their required reserve for creating even more money out of nothing to loan at interest.*

Both sides were able to get rich while the people suffered. The government got all the money it needed for war and the bankers got rich off the infinite interest payments. In reality, these were not real loans, all the bank really did was manufacture money out of nothing, and the government became addicted to the practice of acquiring money without dealing with the unpopular policy of open taxation. As a result, inflation ran out of control because of all this newly created money flooding the economy. Inevitably when runs on the bank began to occur, Parliament nefariously exempted the bank from honoring the worthless paper notes with lawful money. John Galbraith, in his book **"Money: Whence It Came, Where It Went,"** said: *"In 1780, when Lord George Gordon led his mob through London in protest against the Catholic Relief Act, the bank was a principal target. It signified the establishment. For so long as the Catholic districts of London were being pillaged, the authorities were slow to react. When the siege of the bank began, things were thought more serious. Troops intervened and ever since soldiers have been sent to guard the bank by night."* After the end of England's 7 great wars in 1821, along with the bank's reserves, the excuse to print new money ran out as well. The Bank of England was forced to return to a partial gold standard for a short time through the Peel Act of 1844. But there was no way the bankers would allow their profitable scheme of making themselves wealthy by collecting interest on money that they could simply create out of nothing, come to an end. So once again their nefarious puppet politicians were put to work repealing the Peel Act in 1847 and the plunder continued.

This same old union of minds and purpose between the political and monetary scientists has finally come to America under the Federal Reserve System. As long as politicians lack the will to spend within their means and war remains the most lucrative business on this planet, and as long as we the people do not demand a return to sound and fair monetary policy, we will forever be saddled with perpetually expanding debt.

The Rothschilds

By now we should understand why wars are so profitable. We should also understand who financially benefits from wars. Now we must examine the rise of the House of Rothschild and their formula for the instigation of war and its conversion into debt.

This story begins with the birth of Mayer Amschel Bauer in 1743 in Frankfurt, Germany. After learning the family business of "money lending," and working in a bank in Hanover, where he began to perfect his skills before changing his name to Rothschild and returning to take over the family business, Rothschild greatly multiplied his fortune by secretly financing wars in Europe. Mayer Amschel Rothschild had five sons who were set up in the banking business all over Europe. Amschel Mayer, the eldest son, stayed in Frankfurt. Solomon went to Vienna. Nathan went to London. Carl went to Naples. Jacob went to Paris.

Nathan was the cleverest, and demonstrated it when he employed the use of spies to report to him on the outcome of the battle of Waterloo. With the exclusive news that Napoleon had lost, Nathan stood at his usual post in the London exchange, and with a sullen look on his face he began to sell his British stocks. This was a cunning move. What he wanted to do was to trick everyone into believing that it was England that had just lost the war. Everyone knew that if Napoleon defeated England, the first thing he would do is take over the bank and confiscate all securities. Nobody would retain their assets if that happened. So the best thing investors could do if Napoleon won, would be to liquidate their securities in the market. Nathan's Academy Award winning performance paid off; when he started selling, the market followed suit, and the selling panic began. When the market bottomed out, Nathan Rothschild bought everything at a fraction of its worth and cornered the market. He now was the sole collector of all the interest generated by the debt of the British Empire. In one fell-swoop he took control of the Bank of England. Eustace Mullins, in his book, **"The Secrets of the Federal Reserve,"** writes: *"Because of his success in his speculations, Baron Nathan Mayer de Rothschild, as he now called himself, reigned as the supreme financial power in London. He arrogantly exclaimed, during a party in his mansion, 'I care not what puppet is placed upon the throne of England to rule the Empire on which the sun never set. The man that controls Britain's money supply controls the British Empire, and I control the British money supply.'"*

Nathan knew that politicians lack the courage to tax, so they borrow to finance war as well as many other government operations. Privately owned central banks like the Bank of England and her daughter, the Federal Reserve, with their fiat money (money not backed by gold) has guaranteed war as a permanent fixture. In Europe, the Bank of England accomplished this goal and financed 7 different wars, from 1687 until 1812.

To ensure their position as the world's wealthiest family, the Rothschilds marry only within their own family, and only allow family members to hold key positions within their core holdings. As well, they have never allowed a public inventory of their estate. The Cecil Rhodes' monopoly on the South African diamond mines and gold fields, the Harrimans' Railroad empire in the United States and Soviet Manganese production, the Vanderbilts in the railroads and the press, and Andrew Carnegie in the steel industry were all financed by the

Rothschilds. Their capital and financial influence has almost single handedly shaped the rate, pace, and sequence of the development of our modern civilization more than any other calculable medium. Dominating international transactions on behalf of most of the nations of the world, they are the undisputed largest international financiers in recorded history.

J. P. Morgan was their chief agent in America, turning Wall Street into a gigantic Morgan-dominated institution. After the deadly plutocratic brigade of Rothschild agents working in the United States instigated a series of financial panics, culminating with the great financial panic of 1907, the American people demanded monetary reform. Playing this situation like a musical virtuoso, the Rothschilds used these crises to create the leverage necessary for their agents J. P. Morgan, Paul Warburg, and others, to convince the U.S. government that the only way to avoid these types of periods of financial upheaval, would be to create a privately owned central bank in America. The bank would have to be modeled after its mother, the Bank of England. These ignominious aspirations of the Rothschilds' toward economic domination of the world has brought us the Federal Reserve System, and with it, economic slavery and war as a permanent fixture. Congress should abolish the Federal Reserve System now before it's too late.

Chapter Three

Debt Slavery
Comes to America

The Revolutionary War

*T*he privately owned Bank of England had a profound impact in the instigation of the Revolutionary War in America, and to understand it, we must take a look at the economic climate in the pre-Revolutionary American colonies. At that time America was very poor. Not having sufficient precious metal coin to facilitate trade, America began to print its own debt free paper money. The bills would be issued without the backing of gold. It was called Colonial Scrip. This practice proved to be very successful because there was no interest to be paid to a central bank. When the Bank of England demanded Benjamin Franklin to explain how the colonies suddenly began to rapidly prosper, he replied: *"That simple. In the colonies, we issue our own money. It is called Colonial*

Script. We issue it in proper proportion to the demands of trade and industry to make the products pass easily from the producers to the consumers. In this manner creating for ourselves our own paper money, we control its purchasing power, and we have no interest to pay to no one."

The Bank of England viewed America's monetary policies as a threat to their imperial power. Parliament had to do something. They decided to pass the Currency Act of 1764. This restricted the colonies from printing their own money and thereby forced payment of colonial taxes to England in gold or silver coins. The problem with that request is that the pre-Revolutionary colonies were very poor and did not have sufficient gold and silver to make the payments. This new gold standard caused severe economic depression, and ultimately rebellion in the colonies. Benjamin Franklin pointed to this policy as the true reason that America had to go to war with England and declare its independence: *"The colonies would have gladly borne the little tax on tea and other matters had it not been that England took away from the colonies their money, which created unemployment and dissatisfaction. The inability of the colonists to get the power to issue their own money permanently out of the hands of George III and the international bankers was the prime reason for the Revolutionary War."*

England's demand for gold constituted a new gold standard. This was levied upon the colonies by Rothschild agents in the British Parliament through the Currency Act of 1764. This event proves that the gold standard is not necessarily the answer to monetary reform today. Since 1794 nearly all of the critics of the gold standard have highlighted this period to argue the fact that gold's scarcity makes it impossible to fully facilitate trade in an expanding economy. Inconvertible or non-backed notes issued by the people, like colonial script, will work fine, as long as they are issued in exact proportion to the demands of trade during times of peace.

During times of war, as we shall see when we continue to examine the Revolutionary War and subsequent wars in this book, expansion of the amount of currency in circulation is common. It's not rocket science; the greater the increase of currency in circulation, the more that currency is devalued.

The circulation of money within a country is likened unto the circulation of blood within the physical body. Dr. Lee Warren, in the PLIM Report, www.plim.org, said: *"The money supply of a civilization is in many ways analogous to the blood's circulation in the physical body. The blood's circulation is absolutely necessary for the body to have life. Likewise, money must circulate for a civilization to have life or prosperity. If the circulation of the blood is constricted, the individual blacks out or loses consciousness. Likewise, if the money supply of a civilization is contracted, it will literally fall into chaos or an economic depression."* Conversely, if there is too much blood pressure in the body, a stroke is usually the outcome. Likewise, if there is too much money in circulation, the economy experiences a stroke.

The demand for gold in the colonies by the Bank of England caused severe monetary contractions and economic depression. The colonies simply did not have enough gold to meet the bank's demand. War with England was inevitable because of these policies, which is exactly what the Rothschilds and their sinister gang of international financiers wanted. Remember, nothing generates debt like war, and debt generates interest; that's how a bank makes money.

Whether the colonies were able to pay in gold or not, the British government could not allow these American economic ambitions to infect their other colonial territories. The Bank of England stood to lose their imperial control all over the world if America successfully declared economic independence by printing its own money. If this economic insurrection was successful in America, their other territories could decide to do the same thing. Therefore these actions by England went way beyond fleecing; England was also sending the message to all its colonial subjects that nobody challenges the hegemony of the bank.

The Bank of North America

Through guile, treachery, and outright extortion, the Bank of England succeeded in robbing the colonies of their gold and silver coins. But the colonists did not give up their thrust towards independence. Vowing not to be debt slaves to the Bank of England any longer, the American government had no choice; they were forced to print more fiat money (money not backed by gold) to finance the Revolutionary War. The use of fiat money is not necessarily a bad thing. Like Ben Franklin said, as long as the government issues it: *"in proper proportion to the demands of trade and industry to make the products pass easily from the producers to the consumers. In this manner creating for ourselves our own paper money, we control its purchasing power, and we have no interest to pay to no one."* Again, this policy will work fine during times of peace. But during times of war, issuing fiat money to finance the tremendous costs associated with waging war, is almost always inflationary. The colonists found this out in no uncertain terms.

The amount of paper currency in circulation grew from 10 million to over 500 million dollars at the start of the war. This ruined the colonies. The citizens of the colonies not only began to lose faith in this paper money, but also in their government's ability to handle the economy. The politicians were fearful for their jobs and of revolt from the citizenry. They became desperate for monetary reformation. But just like today, not everyone in Congress understood basic monetary science. The British bankers immediately took advantage of the situation and had their agents in the colonial government convince the Congress of the need to establish the first privately owned central bank in America.

By 1781, the Continental Congress became so exasperated with the economy they gave in and allowed the monetary scientists to take over. The Rothschild agents in the Congress hastily went to work establishing the Bank of North America. Now America had its first privately owned central bank, even before the Constitution was drafted. The Bank was organized by a Philadelphia member of Congress named Robert Morris. Rev. Charles A. Goodrich, in his book, *"Lives of the Signers to the Declaration of Independence,"* said that: *"Morris was appointed superintendent of finance by congress, an office then for the first time established. This appointment was unanimous. Indeed it is highly probable that no other man in the country would have been competent to the task of managing such great concerns as it involved, or possessed, like himself, the happy expedient of raising supplies, or deservedly enjoyed more, if equal, public confidence among his fellow-citizens, for punctuality in the fulfillment of his engagements."* Morris was viewed in this very sympathetic light by many people at the time the colonies were suffering the ravages of the depression. Unlike most elected officials of his time and even today, he was a highly skilled monetary scientist. He was considered by his elected peers as the financial wizard of Congress. But later, his true colors would be revealed to all who had inductively decided his character was of true benevolence and patriotism, they would all see that he was more of a plutocrat than a patriot. In reality, Morris was a Rothschild agent who became filthy rich, from war contracts during the Revolution.

The Bank of North America was America's first failed experiment with a privately owned central bank. It was modeled after the Bank of England, with an identical policy in principle of the practice of maintaining a fractional reserve. At that particular time this was necessary because of both the proven impracticality of a gold standard, and the need to help service the expanding debt generated by the war. Therefore Congress made allowances in its charter, albeit under duress, that allowed it to issue paper promissory notes in excess of actual deposits.

The bank was the official depository of all revenue generated by the federal government. It also loaned millions to the government in fractional money (money partially backed by gold). As always with fractional reserve lending, the result was that the money supply became dangerously expanded and massive inflation became a stagnant fixture in the colonies. The situation was so grave that George Washington said: *"A wagon load of money will scarcely purchase a wagon load of provisions ... We may one day become a great commercial and flourishing nation. But if in the pursuit of the means we should unfortunately stumble again on non-funded paper money or any similar specie of fraud, we shall assuredly give a fatal stab to our national credit in its infancy."*

We must remember that the war was still in progress at the time the Bank of North America was conceived, and that elected statesmen follow the course of political expediency. As one legislator named William M. Gouge explained it in his book, ***"A Short History of Paper Money and Banking in the United States"***: *"Do you think, gentlemen, that I will consent to load my constituents with taxes when we can send to our printer and get a wagon load of money, one quire of which will pay for the whole?"*

The resulting lack of confidence in the Bank of North America caused Morris' political power and position to very quickly evaporate. By the end of the war in 1783, just two years after its charter, the first failed experiment with a privately owned central bank in the United States was over; its charter was not renewed.

When the Constitutional Congress convened in Philadelphia in 1787, angry mobs sought regress in the streets. Threats against the lives of government officials were common. Looting was making headlines. Businesses were going bankrupt in record numbers. Public intoxication and contempt for the law was the reactionary response from an unwitting public being fleeced. All because the seeds of fiat money (money not backed by gold) had grown into thorns and thistles, and bore its terrible fruit. And when that bitter fruit ripened, the delegates had to eat it, but did not like its taste.

As economic depression struck, Massachusetts' farmers were increasingly burdened by debt, a problem exacerbated by an increase in taxes. In August 1786, Western Massachusetts farmers organized a violent attempt to shut down three county courthouses in order to prevent foreclosure proceedings. Known as Shay's Rebellion, this uprising was easily put down, but it alerted many to the weaknesses of the government. Although most citizens at the time blamed the Articles of Confederation, the real reason for the economic upheavals was The Bank of North America and its fiat money. The Bank of North America, issuing a flood of these worthless paper notes, nearly destroyed America. George Bancroft, in his book, *"A Plea for the Constitution of the United States,"* tells us that Oliver Ellsworth, the third Chief Justice of the Supreme Court, said: *"This is a favorable moment to shut and bar the door against paper money. The mischief's of the various experiments which have been made are now fresh in the public mind and have excited the disgust of all the respectable parts of America."*

The state of Pennsylvania then chartered the Bank of North America as a commercial bank. Alas, the first privately owned central bank in the history of the United States became known as the First Bank of Pennsylvania. When former Federal Reserve economist, John Bunting, became CEO of First Penn, according to G. Edward Griffin in his book, **"The Creature from Jekyll Island,"** he was the epitome of the unbridled avarice that characterized the era. Griffin said: *"He vastly increased earnings ratios, by reducing safety margins, taking on risky loans, and speculating in the bond market. As long as the economy expanded, these gambles were profitable, and the stockholders loved him dearly. When his gamble in the bond market turned sour, however, the bank plunged into a negative cash flow. By 1979, First Penn was forced to sell off several of its profitable subsidiaries in order to obtain operating funds, and it was carrying $328 million in questionable loans. That was $16 million more than stockholder investment. The bank was insolvent, and the time had arrived to hit up the taxpayers for the loss."* In 1980, the First Bank of Pennsylvania, the oldest and twenty third largest bank in America, following the tradition of the kind of greed that characterized its beginning, had to be bailed out by the FDIC.

The First Bank of the United States

The previous section briefly illustrated a few of the problems created for America in its first failed experiment with a privately owned central bank, the Bank of North America. After its termination, and a brief period of prosperity, the monetary and political scientists worked against the Constitution, the will of Congress, and the best interests of the American people to establish a new privately owned central bank, which would again create money out of nothing to loan to the government at interest, and use the government's IOUs as a financial base.

The proposal for the First Bank of the United States was submitted to Congress in 1790 by Alexander Hamilton, who was at that time, Treasury Secretary and former aid to

Robert Morris. Hamilton showed in his great state papers, both the two *"Reports on Public Credit"* (1790, 1795), as well as in his *"Report on Manufactures"* (1791), and in his *"Report on a National Bank"* (Dec. 13, 1790), that he advocated a private central bank with semipublic functions, patterned after the Bank of England. The intent of these papers was to convince Congress that he possessed a remarkable acquaintance with economic principles as then understood. Most historians have concluded that there was no statesman of the eighteenth century, with the exception of Turgot, who combined more successfully the attributes of a great leader, with the ability to present powerful and sustained reasoning on economic problems, than Alexander Hamilton.

Hamilton and the bank were strongly opposed by Thomas Jefferson. Jefferson never pretended to grasp economic problems, his only contribution to the subject being found in his *"Notes on Virginia"* (1786). These papers prove that Jefferson didn't have a clue about the future industrial development of America. But Jefferson did understand that although it was called the First Bank of the United States, it was still privately owned and an inherently dangerous proposition. He understood enough about how money works to know what causes inflation. He also pointed out that the Constitution did not grant Congress the power to create a bank, and that the issue of America's money, as the Constitution plainly says, should remain with the people. Jefferson said: *"If the American people ever allow private banks to control the issue of their currency, first by inflation, then by deflation, the banks and the corporations that grow up around them will deprive the people of all property until their children wake up homeless on the continent their fathers conquered."* Jefferson also went on to say: *"A private central bank issuing the public currency is a greater menace to the liberties of the people than a standing army ... We must not let our rulers load us with perpetual debt."*

Alexander Hamilton argued that a moderate and manageable debt was good for the country because the national economy was existential in nature. In other words, the nation needed to expand the money supply in order to keep up with expanding commerce. Hamilton went on to paraphrase his argument by saying: *"A national debt if not excessive would be to us a national blessing."* I am forced to ask, who really was the *"us"* Hamilton was referring to? Was it a nation of people whose prolific productivity demanded this perilous escalation of its money supply in order to facilitate its commerce, or was the *"us"* he referred to, in reality, his moneyed confederates in the international banking establishment? I wonder.

After a year of contentious legal and philosophical debate, Alexander Hamilton and his new federalist constituents succeeded in winning this historic debate over Jefferson and his republican constituents. Congress then gave a 20-year charter to the First Bank of the United States. But this bank would be no different than the first private central bank in the colonies, which had not only failed, but had created chaos and economic depression. It was nothing more than a replica of the Bank of North America. Once again another privately owned central bank, the First Bank of the U.S., was given a monopoly on the issue of bank notes. The First Bank of the U.S. was also owned by the same private investors that owned the Bank of North America and the Bank of England. Biographer, Derek Wilson, in his book *"**The Rothschilds**,"* explained how the Rothschild banking dynasty in Europe was the dominant force behind America's central banks, both financially and politically. He explains: *"Nathan Rothschild was a pledged supporter of the Bank of the U.S."* Gustavus Myers, in his book, **"The History of Great American Fortunes,"** said: *"Under the surface, the Rothschilds' long had a powerful influence in dictating American financial laws. The law records show that they were the power in the old Bank of the United States."*

The First Bank of the United States' policy of fractional reserve banking did the same thing to America's economy that the Bank of North America's utilization of the printing press to add to the money supply did; it caused inflation to run rampant, and it ruined the American economy and generated an enormous amount of debt. To this end, Thomas Jefferson said: *"I wish it were possible to obtain a single amendment to our Constitution ... I mean an additional article, taking from the Federal government their power of borrowing."*

By 1814, Americans were finally fed up. They woke up and began to demand their gold instead of paper money. The Bank of the United States, America's second experiment with a privately owned central bank, had failed. That bank, like the first one, became the ultimate instrument of plutocracy, or rule by the rich, robbing the American people out of 66% of their wealth, on top of the 42% Americans lost with the Bank of North America. Today, the torch of plutocracy has been passed to the Federal Reserve.

The Second Bank of the United States

The bankers and politicians who profited from the First Bank of the United States, which was America's second failed experiment with a privately owned central bank, were still influenced and controlled by their benefactors within the European banking aristocracy. These European aristocrats had tasted the spoils of their colonial conquests in the new world, and they liked it. Their greed goes way beyond mere money; power is what they crave. My brother, Broward County Commissioner Josephus Eggelletion Jr., once told me during his freshman tenure in the Florida House of Representatives, of the need to remain humble in public office: *"If you allow it, power can become an aphrodisiac."* He was echoing the sentiments of John F. Kennedy in his October 26, 1963 speech at Amherst College: *"The men who create power make an indispensable contribution to the Nation's greatness, but the men who question power make a contribution just as indispensable, especially when that questioning is disinterested, for they determine whether we use power or power uses us.* When influential men succumb to the lesser angels of their nature, and sell their souls to acquire power, the poor should take cover. In the case of England's desire to maintain an unchallenged imperial position in the development of the Americas, they would never give up on the permanent placement of their most powerful tool of imperial control—private central banks in America under their dominant influence and control. As Jefferson said: *"A private central bank issuing the public currency is a greater menace to the liberties of the people than a standing army ... We must not let our rulers load us with perpetual debt."* Most people do not understand that controlling a nation's money and credit is a powerful weapon against the sovereignty of its people, and economic weapons are just as devastating as nuclear weapons.

But because some politicians know about as much about monetary policy as a silverback gorilla does about Einstein's Theory of Special Relativity, the scientists of money have always made fools of the politicians and the people. In 1816, the bewildered members of the U.S. Congress granted a 20-year charter to the Second Bank of the United States. The fact that the new bank was a carbon copy of the old bank, the fact that one third of its stock was owned by investors in England, and the fact that we had been there and done that before, didn't register a red flag in their minds. Too bad JFK wasn't around to tell them that the *"men who create power make an indispensable contribution to the Nation's greatness."* But they probably would have murdered him at that time as well.

By 1818 the states were also getting into the act, chartering new banks at a record pace of 50% more than the previous years. Using the principle of fractional reserve banking, these new state banks, along with the Second Bank of the United States, expanded the nation's money supply by an additional 27.4 million dollars. This amounted to the transfer of over 40% of the wealth of the people through this expansion of the money supply. Understand this: when the money supply is rapidly expanded like that, it subsequently creates an invisible tax, commonly called inflation. Then through a feeble attempt to correct the damage done by inflation, at that time the banks deliberately contracted the money supply, creating deflation, the situation was made even worse.

Jackson and No Bank

It took just a little more than a decade for the American people to once again lose faith in their government's ability to handle the economy. The country was fed up and finally demanded a sound monetary system. They wanted nothing else to do with the First Bank of the United States. By this time, the Republicans had abandoned the Jeffersonian ideology, and a new Democratic Party had been established, headed by Andrew Jackson and Martin Van Buren.

In 1819, President Monroe appointed Nicholas Biddle as one of the directors of the Second Bank of the United States. By 1823 Biddle had become its president. Like Robert Morris and Alexander Hamilton, Biddle was able to convince the naive members of Congress of the necessity for a private central banking institution to stabilize the currency and curb the tendencies toward inflation in the economy.

Biddle was the son of a wealthy Philadelphia family, and was well versed in the science of money. Using the bank's privilege to operate branches in many states, Biddle built the institution into the most powerful banking house in the United

States. After Andrew Jackson won the presidency in 1828, he began to try to get Congress to dissolve the Second Bank of the United States, making Biddle the leading target of the Jacksonians in their war against the bank. Upon realizing that the bank was in danger of losing its charter, Biddle fought the Jacksonians constantly as he guided the Second Bank of the U.S., beginning in 1823, throughout the bitter conflict with Andrew Jackson over the bank's charter. Although Biddle got the Congress to pass the legislation which would re-charter the bank early, President Jackson vetoed the bill. Jackson would not tolerate the fleecing of America by a predominately foreign plutocratic influence. He clearly understood the unconstitutionality of this government-sponsored monopoly for what it really was—a threat to America's strategic national security. Jackson exclaimed: *"Controlling our currency, receiving our public monies, and holding thousands of our citizens in dependence, it would be more formidable and dangerous than a naval and military power of the enemy."*

The historical account of the epic battle between Nicholas Biddle and Andrew Jackson is generally glossed over in high school and college history courses. I have found it to have been truly one of the most monumental events in American history, and more than worthy of being spotlighted in this book. Specifically, Biddle managed to buy Congress, the banks, speculators, industrialists, segments of the press, and even the great Senator Daniel Webster. But Jackson, through an appeal to the voters, and campaigning on the slogan *"Jackson and no bank,"* won re-election and continued to fight both Biddle and the bank. Making an analogy to the great mythological battle between Hercules and the Hydra, Jackson was quoted as saying: *"The hydra of corruption is only scotched, not dead."* In a tactical attempt to drain and kill the bank, Jackson then ordered the removal of government deposits from the bank. In a draconian retaliatory response,

Biddle decided to contract the money supply and cause economic panic in an attempt to get the public to blame Jackson's deposit removal policy for the panic, which would force Jackson out of the way. Biddle's response bought him a little time, because the whole country then began to blame Jackson for the financial crisis. As a result, the Senate censored Jackson. President Jackson then threatened the bankers: *"You are a den of vipers, I intend to root you out and by the Eternal God I will root you out!"* Biddle's downfall began when he started to boast about how he deliberately crippled the economy. He then refused to let the affairs of the bank be audited by Congress. This act of arrogance, along with the fact that Jackson eventually paid off the national debt with a surplus to spare for the construction of various public works, sealed Biddle's fate. Congress decided not to renew the bank's charter in 1836. Biddle was arrested and charged with fraud. The next time a surplus would be amassed by a president would be during the Clinton administration in the late 1990s.

It is not surprising that there was an assassination attempt on Jackson's life on January 30, 1835. As Jackson himself said: *"The bank is trying to kill me, but I will kill it."* But in spite of attempts on Jackson's life and the economic life of all Americans, President Andrew Jackson's life and the nation's economy were spared. In fact, Jackson won the fight and balanced the federal budget in 1835. Historians have counted it as one of the greatest presidential achievements in history.

The battle between Andrew Jackson and Nicholas Biddle was a continuation of a centuries old economic Cold War between bankers and patriotic elected officials. The Second Bank of the United States was America's third failed experiment with a privately owned central bank. Beware: the Federal Reserve is the fourth.

ANDRE MICHAEL EGGELLETION

Government Monetary Reforms

Fed up with the ravages of fiat money (money un-backed by gold), in April 1836 the government nearly abandoned paper currency, and began to require the use of gold and silver coin. Paper money transactions were largely restricted to large denominations of paper money, which were used for larger commercial transactions and bank transfers. This was the beginning of the concept of "Hard Money" in 19th century America. In spite of its inherent fairness in terms of being based on a system of honesty in weights and measures (each coin containing an honest and fair amount of precious metal), hard money failed for the same reason its use is not standard today. It failed because most banks at that time made transactions using checks and their book entries. Today these types of transactions are done by computers. So abandoning paper money in smaller denominations was like putting a bandage on cancer. At best, the hard money practice became inconsequential.

The monetary and political scientists then began to try to base their bank notes on bank assets. The problem with that was the fact that these assets were largely intangible. Most of the assets of the banks were merely checkbook entries—numbers in a ledger—and since they still operated according to the fractional reserve principle, inflation was the result. The problem remained.

During the crisis of 1837 the bankers were desperate to come up with a solution to the danger that the inflationary aspects of fractional reserve banking had created among them. The plan was to get the politicians to endorse the concept of an insurance fund that would organize the mutual support of banks by each other. This was the forerunning model that prefigured the FDIC. It too failed. In the 1850s, they tried to base money on government securities or bonds, which are nothing more than government tax backed debt certificates. It failed. Next they came up with a proposal to back the money supply with state-based credit. It failed.

Some contemporary monetary scientists have tried to blame Andrew Jackson's termination of the Second Bank of the U.S. as the reason for the 1837 Panic. They say that we must have privately owned central banks to handle our monetary policy, and point to the 1837 Panic to justify that position. I strongly disagree with them; all these pre-Civil War monetary reform measurers failed because of the same thing— fractional reserve banking always leads to inflation. History screams at us to learn that anytime you give bankers the power to create money out of nothing and loan it back to the government at interest, they are going to expand the money supply until the money in circulation becomes worthless. Fractional reserve banking laws are nothing more than a license to inflict great harm on a nation through the unbridled avarice of a handful of men.

Not only do I disagree with their indictments of Andrew Jackson, but so does Peter Temin, of the MIT Department of Economics. Temin argues that the inflation of the money supply that led to the 1837 Panic was created by a massive inflow of silver into the U.S. during that time. This would have increased the reserve ratios of banks, allowing them to make more loans, thereby increasing the money supply. In an essay by Gareth Davis, Senior Sophister of the University of Dublin School of Mathematics, Davis recalls that Peter Temin "... *backs his argument up by showing how this inflow [of silver] in the 1830s would have resulted from increased silver production in Mexico, from an increase in British investment in America and from the fall in US imports of opium from China, which stopped the outflow of silver. So it is possible to dismiss the relationship between the Bank's demise and the panic of*

1837 as a coincidence." In other words, the absence of a privately owned central bank in America had nothing to do with the creation of the Panic of 1837.

So let's add all of this up. First you have a debased currency because of the fractional reserve policies of the Second Bank of the United States. Then you have the subsequent inflation of that debauched currency because of massive inflows of silver into the American banking system. Finally you have the spineless nature of the average politician's propensity to borrow rather than tax. All of that adds up to a recipe for a financial panic in 1837.

We should have learned by now that fractional reserve banking is dangerous. But I think that it is a practice that will likely always be around, because it allows politicians to borrow us into oblivion in order to satisfy their benefactors in the corporate and banking world. If levying taxes was the only way to raise revenue no politician would be willing to risk the wrath of the voters for overspending, you can take a monkey and knock his brains out and he should be able to see that.

Another unfortunate by-product of the political mandate to borrow the nation into debt, thereby expanding the deficit, is that debt and deficits always lead to economic depression and social unrest. During this pre-Civil War period, America tried everything except the full backing of its money supply in gold and silver. But as long as there are wars, there will always be a need for capitalization that goes beyond the strict and rudimentary limitations of a gold standard.

We have seen how money can help or hurt a society. By having too much in circulation inflation is created. Not having enough creates recession and depression. We should now briefly review and examine money and its different forms.

Different Forms of Money

Money itself is defined as anything used as a medium of exchange for purchase of goods, payment of debts, and to facilitate trade. Money can also be defined as an evidence of debt owed by a society. Eugene Kline, in his book *"Money and Banking"* characterizes the differences between these first and second definitions of money. He starts with the second as being: *"useful in understanding the basic nature and character. It is much less precise than the first, however, for it includes in addition to money many other evidences of debt such as bonds, debentures, promissory notes, mortgages and savings passbooks. The first definition helps determine the line between money and near-money. When one is studying, for instance, the effects of changes in the money supply, it is necessary to know just what may be counted as money."*

Based upon this protocol, let us briefly examine the nature of the four primary types of money, so that we might come to a workable understanding of how changes in the money supply can adversely affect our quality of life.

Commodity Money: Commodity money was first used in modern history in the form of precious metals. Experience has demonstrated to a large extent that precious metals are the only reliable base for an honest monetary system when measured and weighed to exact standards. This is why the bible records the required use of honesty in weights, measures, and scales. (Deut. 25:13-15, Prov. 11:1, Rom. 12:17, James 5:4, Ex. 20:15)

Receipt Money: Receipt money is simply a paper note, or similar specie which represents an equal amount of precious metal or something of intrinsic value. This is what early Federal Reserve notes were. Written on the notes was the inscription "Redeemable in lawful money." In other words, the bearer of those notes could redeem them at any Federal Reserve Bank for precious metal coins in the amount of the full face value of the note being redeemed. Today that inscription has been removed, and the reference to redeemable in lawful money no longer has any significance.

Fractional Money: Paper money is only partially backed by precious metals. Fractional money is a lower or debased form of receipt money. The sanctioning of fractional money as legal tender is the pathway to ruin. As G. Edward Griffin points out in ***"The Creature from Jekyll Island":*** *"Generally, the public is unaware of this fact, and believes that fractional money can be redeemed at any time. When the truth is discovered, as periodically happens, there are runs on the bank, and only the first few depositors in line can be paid."* Griffin goes on to conclude that *"Fractional money will always degenerate into fiat money. It is but fiat money in transition."*

Fiat Money: Fiat money is paper money or notes without the backing of precious metals at all. Metal coins without gold or silver content that are not backed by precious metals is also a form of fiat money. Fiat money is totally worthless. It is only backed up by the faith of the people of the government in which it is issued. Again, we turn to G. Edward Griffin in ***"The Creature from Jekyll Island"*** for his analysis. He said that fiat money *"allows politicians to increase spending without raising taxes. Fiat money is the cause of inflation, and the amount that people lose in purchasing power is exactly the amount which was taken from them and transferred to their government in this process. Inflation, therefore, is a hidden tax. This tax is the most unfair of all because it falls most heavily on those least able to pay: the small wage earner, and those on fixed incomes. It also punishes the thrifty by eroding the value of their savings. This creates resentment among the people, leading always to political unrest and national* *disunity ... A nation that resorts to the use of fiat money had doomed itself to economic hardship and political disunity."* This is the form of money that we have in America today through the Federal Reserve System.

Chapter Four

Divide and Conquer

The Civil War

*H*istory has taught us that slavery was the issue over which the Civil War was fought. This is not entirely true; wars are very complex things, with many reasons for their genesis. There are geo-political, strategic, economic, hegemonic, colonial, and imperial elements to be considered when evaluating why wars are fought. The Civil War, like every other war, was spawned for a variety of reasons that took many years to materialize. Some of these reasons were of a national origin, and some of these reasons were of international origin.

For the purpose of this book, I do not intend to rehearse the events that led to the Civil War in polytechnic detail. But first of all, dispense with the assertion that slavery was the sole reason for the dissolution of the union, and allow me to illuminate the economic forces that were working to divide and conquer America. Frankly, to believe that slavery was the sole reason that the union was almost permanently divided would be naïve. If one wishes to reduce the genesis of war to one specific cause, the most consistent common denominator would be money. But we will never understand the true nature of the Civil War's materialization without understanding the motives of the international banking establishment. But if you still want to believe that slavery was the prime reason for the Civil War then you don't want to believe Lincoln's stated position on the issue. President Lincoln said in his 1st inaugural address: *"I have no purpose, directly or indirectly, to interfere with the institution of slavery in the states where it now exists. I believe I have no lawful right to do so, and I have no inclination to do so."* On the question of Lincoln's humanistic benevolence towards the Negro, in his fourth debate with Stephen Douglas he said: *"I am not nor ever have been in favor of bringing about in any way the social and political equality of the white and the black races—that I am not nor ever have been in favor of making voters or jurors of Negroes, nor of qualifying them to hold office, to marry with white people; and I will say in addition to this that there is a physical difference between the white and black races which I believe will forever forbid the two races from living together on terms of social and political equality. And in as much as they cannot so live, while they do remain together there must be the position of superior and inferior, and I as much as any other man am in favor of having the superior position assigned to the white race."* In his own words, there Lincoln defines himself as a white supremacist.

So what were the true mitigating factors, besides slavery, that led to the Civil War? If the war was fought for the purpose of preserving the union, why did the union need preserving? For what reason did the South choose to secede?

The scarcely told truth of the matter is that the war's motive was an irreconcilable conflict of economic interests, which included slavery, between the North and South. The South wanted cheaper goods produced in Europe, thus bringing harm to Northern industrialists. The North retaliated, placing high export taxes on the South's cotton, thus bringing harm to Southern agriculturalists. Adding insult to the injury being inflicted upon the South by the North, Europe reacted by not purchasing the South's cotton. On top of all that, add the pressure to end slavery, and the potential European financial gains in a divided America unable to enforce her Monroe Doctrine, and war became inevitable.

So who or what malefic force in Europe's financial establishment was seeking to profit from a divided America? It was none other than the same Rothschild family that plunged England into war. They were and still are the masters of international finance through the instigation, manipulation, and exploitation of war. Remember, history has recorded that nothing generates the need for capitalization (finance through borrowing) like war does. This is why the Rothschilds were now instigating war in America. By secretly financing and creating debtors of both sides in America, the Rothschilds and the international bankers stood to rob the people of both sides. They didn't care who won the war, they were only interested in dividing America so that they could control the pace and sequence of the development of the American frontier, for their own gain.

But Abraham Lincoln was unwilling to saddle America with the type of debt that the international bankers had in mind. He absolutely refused to finance the war with Rothschild money because of the unreasonable 27.5 percent interest they wanted. Not knowing how he would finance the war effort, Lincoln needed the advice of some one that he could trust, someone who was motivated by their convictions against slavery on moral grounds, and not merely the tactical ground to which he himself was only concerned. Thank heaven there was a member of the war department at that time who possessed that kind of heart and mind. These were the qualities that were known throughout the nation to be found in his Treasury Secretary, Salmon P. Chase.

Lincoln had the type of confidante he needed in Chase because he knew that Chase, unlike himself, genuinely abhorred the institution of slavery, and wanted to see it abolished as a matter of principle. Chase brought the true perspective of an abolitionist to his post in the War Department. He never refused to help fugitive slaves or people indicted for aiding the escape of slaves. Appearing in defense of many fugitives he never won a case but his fervent efforts made him a friend and counselor to distressed African American slaves in Ohio and all over the country. As an attorney, taking on these cases brought little else but publicity. He was seldom paid for his services and may have lost clients due to his association with the blacks and abolitionists. At some anti-slavery rallies Chase was pelted with eggs, on one occasion he was even hit with a brick.

To show their strong sense of gratitude for Chase's defense of Samuel Watson, a runaway slave, and for his other undertakings on behalf of slaves, he was presented with a sterling silver pitcher, by the Colored People of Cincinnati, as a testimonial of gratitude for his efforts in the Watson case and for other services. The pitcher bore the following inscription: A testimonial of gratitude to "SALMON P. CHASE FROM THE COLORED PEOPLE OF CINCINNATI, for his various public services in behalf of the oppressed and particularly for his ELOQUENT ADVOCACY OF THE RIGHTS OF MAN" in the case of Samuel Watson, who was claimed as a fugitive slave, Feb. 12, 1845. Daniel A. P. Murray, in his *"African-American Pamphlets from the Daniel A. P. Murray Collection 1880-1920,"* records the quote of Chase accepting the gift and stating the beliefs from which he was never to waver: *"True democracy makes no inquiry about the color of the skin, or the places of nativity, or any other similar circumstances of condition. Whenever it sees a man, it recognizes a being endowed by his Creator with original inalienable rights ... I regard, therefore, the exclusion of colored people from the election franchise as incompatible with true democratic principles."*

Lincoln knew that the crusading Chase wanted nothing in this world more than to win the war and end slavery. So when Chase encouraged Lincoln to issue his own currency, declare it to be legal tender and the people will have no other choice but to trade with it, he knew this would enable Lincoln to go ahead and win the war. If we could have such a brave president now, whose policy was that we issue our own money to finance the War on Terrorism, there would be no debt generated by that war. If he would then insist on continuing the policy of government-issued currency after the war, we could use it to pay off the national debt and abolish privately owned central banks in America. That was President Lincoln's exact plan.

So Lincoln began to print his own currency called Greenbacks. The shockwaves throughout the halls of high finance that this action created were tremendous. The international bankers were furious because not only did the Greenbacks not bear any interest for the bankers, Lincoln actually went on to win the war with them. Then Lincoln wanted to continue the Greenback policy after the war was over. This policy would ensure that America would remain the one obstacle to a one-world government. The bankers simply couldn't allow it. A unified America was a formidable impediment to the universal global empire that European bankers envisioned. G. Edward Griffin, in his book, *"The Creature from Jekyll Island,"* indicates that the tactical goal of the international bankers during the middle 19th century was to divide and conquer America. Griffin tells us of remarks by Otto Von Bismark, chancellor of Germany, which confirms this view: *"The division of the United States into federations of equal force was decided long before the Civil War by the high financial powers of Europe. These bankers were afraid that the United States, if they remained as one block, and as one nation, would attain economic and financial independence, which would upset their plans for financial domination of the world."*

Because of the need for more Greenbacks to finance the war, Lincoln had no choice but to return to the inflationary practice of fractional reserve banking. Lincoln agreed to allow Congress to establish the National Banking Act on February 25, 1863. The money supply in the North increased by 138 percent and as a result the Greenbacks value dropped by 65 percent. The South was forced to do the same thing, but with a far greater negative effect on their money. Confederate notes were increased by 214 percent in the South. The South was destroyed militarily and economically as prices rose 9000 percent. Seeing this kind of economic carnage hit Lincoln like a ton of bricks. In the book, *"The Wit and Wisdom of Abraham Lincoln,"* by James C. Humes, the author includes a quote from one of Lincoln's private letters, now known to posterity, which shows how Lincoln came to fully understand the destructive power of fractional reserve banking: *"The money power preys upon the nation in times of peace and conspires against it in times of adversity. It is more despotic than monarchy, more insolent than autocracy, more selfish than bureaucracy. I see in the near future a crisis approaching that unnerves me and causes me to tremble for the safety of my country. Corporations have been enthroned, an era of corruption will follow, and the money power of the country will endeavor to prolong its reign by working upon the prejudices of the people, until the wealth is aggregated in a few hands, and the republic destroyed."*

The Assassination of Abraham Lincoln

The world has been taught that the reason John Wilkes Booth killed Lincoln was as a retaliatory gesture on behalf of the South. Well that would make Booth the dumbest man in America. Booth was not an ignorant man; he was highly educated and politically astute. He was, however, a white supremacist, but in the 1960s so were most white men, including Abraham Lincoln himself. He was known throughout the nation to be the most famous and brilliant actor of his time. Booth killing Lincoln would be like an academy award-winning actor killing the president today.

Lincoln was virtually the only friend that the South had in the union. After the war, the Northern industrialists wanted to plunder the South. The northern politicians wanted to politically disenfranchise, and virtually silence the Southern elected officials in Congress. The War Department wanted to round up every secessionist in the country and execute every last one of them. Lincoln campaigned on a promise to welcome the South back into the union after the war, and never wavered. Even after the war, with tremendous pressure on him to cave in to the vitriolic demands of his War Department, Lincoln, in his words, wanted *"no more killing."* In a speech in Cincinnati, Ohio on September 17, 1859, Lincoln echoed his benevolence to his Southern neighbors saying: *"When we do as we say, beat you, you perhaps want to know what we will do with you. I will tell you, so far as I am authorized to speak for the opposition, what we mean to do with you, we mean to treat you as near as we possibly can, as Washington, Jefferson, and Madison treated you. We mean to leave you alone, and in no way to interfere with your institution* [slavery]*; to abide by all and every compromise of the Constitution, and, in a word, coming back to the original proposition, to treat you, so far as degenerated men (if we have degenerated) may, according to the example of those noble fathers—Washington, Jefferson, and Madison. We mean to remember that you are as good as we; that there is no difference between us other than the difference of circumstances. We mean to recognize and bear in mind always that you have as good hearts in your bosoms as other people, or as we claim to have, and treat you accordingly. We mean to marry your girls when we have a chance—-the white ones, I mean, and I have the honor to inform you that I once did have a chance in that way."* Lincoln framed his second inaugural address, in Washington DC on March 4, 1865, around the theme, "with malice towards none" saying: *"With malice toward none; with charity for all; with firmness in the right, as god gives us to see the right, let us strive on to finish the work we are in; to bind up the nation's wounds; to care for him who shall have borne the battle, and for his widow, and his orphan—to do all which may achieve and cherish a just and lasting peace, among ourselves and with all nations."* Now you have to ask yourself the question, why would a brilliant man like Booth kill the goose that was trying to lay a golden egg for him?

So did monetary policy play a role in the assassination of Abraham Lincoln? The answer is yes. In his book, ***"The Creature from Jekyll Island,"*** G. Edward Griffin points out that Lincoln's economic policies and his *"malice towards none"* policy with the South after the war, made Lincoln's removal attractive. Griffin points out that: *"Running throughout these cross-currents of motives and special interests were two groups which found it increasingly to their advantage to* *have Lincoln out of the way. One group consisted of the financiers, Northern industrialists and radical Republicans, all of whom wanted to legally plunder the South at the end of the war. The other group was smaller in size but equally dangerous. It consisted of hot head confederate sympathizers from both the North and South – who sought revenge."*

It has been suggested that the Knights of the Golden Circle, which was a forerunner of the Ku Klux Klan, and at that time had close ties to the Illuminati in Europe, had one of its members, John Wilkes Booth, a 33rd degree Mason, kill Lincoln. This assertion came from the granddaughter of Booth. She went on to claim that the government covered up Booth's involvement with the international bankers. The book, **"Lincoln Money Martyred,"** by Dr. R. E. Search, tells us that a Canadian newspaper in the 1930s obtained information that was dubiously withheld at Booth's trial after his death and wrote: *"Abraham Lincoln the martyred emancipator of the slaves was assassinated through the machinations of a group representative of the international bankers who feared the U.S. Presidents' national credit ambitions. There was only one group who had any reason to desire the death of Lincoln. They were the men who were opposed to his national currency program and who fought him through the whole Civil War on his policy of Greenback currency, which remained in circulation in the U.S. until 1994 as United States notes."*

The primary reason for the Civil War was not what the academic world has sanctioned as the truth. As we have seen, both the Revolutionary War and the Civil War were instigated by bankers for the purpose of establishing privately owned central banks in America, thus making debtors of her people through the sullen art of usury. We should note that even in the bible usury is forbidden (Deut. 23:19, Lev. 25:35-37, Proverbs 22:16) In the book, **"The Federal Reserve Hoax,"** by W. B. Vennard, the situation of national economic retardation through debt is explained: *"No nation can control its affairs if it cannot control its financial system. As the body of an individual is dependent on blood that flows in its arteries and veins, so does the body politic depend on money, the blood of civilization, that flows in the arteries and veins of its commercial life. It is self-evident. So, to build a political organism, a body politic, which can analyze and master the problem of civilization, we must have control of our financial system, free from interference by the people of any foreign nation."*

The Post-Civil War Era

Just as America had declared her economic independence during the Revolutionary War, America had done it again during the Civil War. These nationalistic monetary policy decisions brought both great prosperity and eventually great adversity to this nation. These policies were made possible only because there were stronger sentiments of nationalism within the government during both of these periods in American history, and those sentiments were far more resilient, than they are today. In spite of the risk of creating and facing a dangerous confrontational posture within the international banking establishment toward America, we had the intestinal fortitude to rise to the occasion and throw off the shackles of economic totalitarianism. Each time America began to figure out that controlling her own money supply was the solution to her economic problems, and began issuing her own money, the international bankers lost a fortune in interest payments that their debt-based currency had been generating. So just like colonial script, Lincoln's Greenbacks were an open challenge to the imperial and hegemonic aspirations of the European international bankers. His decision to continue the Greenback policy after the war cost him his life. To ensure failure of any government momentum toward a government-controlled monetary policy, this time, the bankers fought back with the tenacity of a cornered wild animal.

In a tactical economic response to America's lofty ambitions toward financial independence, the international bankers implemented a forty year long period of harsh recurring monetary restriction in America. They contracted the money supply four times in post-Civil War America, creating the financial panics of 1873, 1884, 1893, and 1907. This monetary policy was designed to ensure that Americans would be so disoriented and battered by economic upheaval that they would accept whatever monetary policy their poodles in government would offer. In order to successfully steer America toward another privately owned central bank, this response would have to be as harmful as possible, and it was. Many people suffered at the hands of these moneyed vultures; farms were lost, families starved, development faltered, businesses failed, personal bankruptcy reached all new highs, and a stagnating economic malaise plagued America. An exposé entitled, **"The History of Money and Private Central Bank Ownership by Freemason/Zionists Mafia,"** by Alexander James, tells us that when James Garfield was elected President in 1880, he publicly denounced their deeds: "Whosoever controls the volume of money in any country is absolute master of all industry and commerce. And when you realize that the entire system is easily controlled, one way or another, by a few powerful men at the top, you will not have to be told how periods of inflation and depression originate." On July 2, 1881, President James Garfield was brutally assassinated.

The Rise of J.P. Morgan

John Pierpont Morgan's story begins with the rise of his father, international investment banker genius, Junius Spencer Morgan. J. S. Morgan was absolutely prolific in the science of investment banking and brokering big money deals in New York City. His rise to international prominence began after becoming a partner in mercantile firms in Hartford and Boston. His star really began to rise in 1854, after moving to London and becoming a partner of George Peabody. Peabody, who achieved enormous international success as an investment banker in London, and was considered by many to be the founder of modern philanthropy, was really a lieutenant for the Rothschilds. It was there in London that J. S. Morgan spent the next ten years being groomed with Peabody and others to broker British concerns. After assuming control of the entire firm, Morgan returned to America in 1854 to change the company's name to J. S. Morgan & Co. Under this new name he began to expand the firm's international banking enterprise into handling British funds invested in the United States. His organization's $50 million loan to the French government at the time of the Franco-Prussian War was one of the largest international banking transactions of the era. J. S. Morgan became the most influential lieutenant in the Rothschild stable of front men.

In 1880, after making a fortune brokering America's war bonds in England during the Civil War, J. S. Morgan was mysteriously killed in a carriage accident. That's when his son, John Pierpont Morgan, took over his father's London-based firm. Educated in Boston and Germany, he honed his skills as an accountant at the New York banking firm of Duncan, Sherman and Company. In 1867, J. P. Morgan transferred to his father's banking company, and ten years later became a partner in Drexel, Morgan and Company. After Drexel's death the company was reorganized as J. P. Morgan and Company in 1895, making it one of the most important banking houses in the world. Guided by the banking and monetary scientists in Europe, in 1898 he expanded and solidified the scope of his father's company as a powerful proxy asset for the Rothschild

British aristocracy. J. P. Morgan was now the most powerful banker in America.

Some of the deals that helped to make J. P. Morgan were the 1891 Morgan-brokered merger of Edison General Electric and Thompson-Houson Electric Company to form General Electric. General Electric then went on to become the largest electrical-equipment manufacturing company in the United States. Steel production was another essential component in America's industrial revolution, and J. P. Morgan was its primary broker. After financing the creation of the Federal Steel Company he joined with Henry Frick to merge Federal Steel with the Carnegie Steel Company to form the United States Steel Corporation. Morgan's connections with the London financial establishment was so deeply entrenched that he was able to broker the lion's share of capitalization for nearly all of the growing industrial corporations in the United States.

Most people believe that it was Morgan's money that provided this funding. That perception is false. That's the perception that the bankers wanted the American people and their elected officials to have. Had the America people realized that Morgan simply brokered these deals with money from British bankers, they would have realized that America was not the sovereign enterprise that they thought it was. They would realize that America was becoming the debt slave of the British international banking aristocracy, and was being led by the Rothschilds. That's why the bankers hand picked J. P. Morgan to become a member of the board of directors in several of these companies, including most of the major railroad companies; his contributions to corporate America made his confirmation to these posts a foregone conclusion. By 1902 Morgan controlled over 5,000 miles of American railroads. J. P. Morgan, more than any other man, during his heyday, was responsible for brokering the capital that enabled the Industrial Revolution in America at the turn of the century.

I repeat, though he financed America's leading Industrial giants, the Rockefellers and the Harrimans, he was only a front for Baron Nathan Mayer Rothschild in America. His Rothschild association was never fully and finally revealed until he died in 1913. People were shocked to learn that his estate was only valued at $68 million—a fraction of the fortunes of the Vanderbilts, Astors and Rockefellers. The bulk of the great fortune that he amassed was held by the Rothschilds. As G. Edward Griffin puts it: *"The possibilities are obvious that a major portion of the wealth and power of the Morgan firm was, and always had been, merely the wealth and power of the Rothschilds who had raised it up in the beginning and who sustained it through its entire existence."*

Lyndon LaRouche Jr. in his book, **"Dope Inc.,"** tells us that on February 5, 1891, a secret association known as the "Round Table Group" was formed in London by Cecil Rhodes, with the backing of his banker, Lord Rothschild, along with Lord Rosebery and Lord Curzon. He went on to state that, in the United States: *"the Round Table was represented by the Morgan Group."* Formed for the purpose of creating the necessary political and economic apparatus, which would operate behind the scenes, they were front organizations for powerful international financiers in London to control, exploit, and redistribute America's wealth into their coffers. Dr. Carol Quigley, in his book, **"Tragedy and Hope,"** refers to this group as *"The British-American Secret Society"* stating that: *"The chief backbone of this organization grew up along the already existing financial corporation running from the Morgan bank in New York to a group of international financiers in London led by Lagard Brothers (in 1901)."* Quigley went on to indicate that the goals of the Round Table Groups throughout the world could not and would not be predicated on a nationalistic or patriotic agenda; the ruling class elite are not restrained from plunder by such inconsequential propaganda. Nationalism and patriotism, in their eyes, are nothing more than an anesthesia for the consciousness of the masses. Quigley writes: *"This network which we may identify as the Round Table Groups, has no aversion to cooperating with the communists, or any other groups, and frequently does so."* Confirming his view, G. Edward Griffin writes: *"The concept that a ruling party or class is the ideal structure for society is at the heart of all collectivists schemes, regardless of whether they are called Socialism, Communism, Nazism, Fascism, or any other 'ism' which may yet be invented to disguise it. It is easy, therefore, for adherents of this elitist mentality to be comfortable in almost any of these collectivist camps."*

The bottom line is that the proponents of privately owned central banks, historically, have been like vultures preying on the wealth of the unwitting masses because of the dead state of our patriotic activism. To this end, Quigley writes that their goal is *"... nothing less than to create a world system of financial control in private hands able to dominate the political system of each country and the economy of the world as a whole. This system was to be controlled in a feudalist fashion by the central banks of the world acting in concert, by secret agreements arrived at in frequent private meetings and conferences."* The American Round Table Group was the forerunner of the Council on Foreign Relations and the Trilateral Commission, which we will discuss later.

The main point to consider at this juncture is the fact that it was the British exploitation of America, through their chief proxy, J. P. Morgan, who dominated interests on Wall Street, and created a perilous financial climate in America after the Civil War. It was their havoc in the American economy which led to the public outcries for monetary reform. Their ultimate plan was to give America another privately owned central bank, issuing an inflationary fiat currency. The chaos they inspired was a means to that end. The private central bank they would create would be called the Federal Reserve.

Booms, Busts, and Panic:
America under the Hegelian Dialectic

The creation of the Federal Reserve System was the debatable solution offered to America by J. P. Morgan's men to deal with a volatile period of financial panics. There were 12 major financial panics in American history: the William Duer Panic in 1792, The Crisis of the Jacksonians Finances in 1837, The Western Blizzard Panic of 1857, The Post-Civil War Panic from 1865-69, The Crisis of the Gilded Age, in 1873, Grant's Last Panic in 1884, Grover Cleveland and the Ordeal of 1893-95, The Northern Pacific Comer of 1901, The Knickerbockers Trust Panic of 1907, Europe Goes to War in 1914, The Great Crash of 1929, and the Kennedy Slide of 1962.

All of these financial panics, whether contrived or occurring naturally, were used by greedy individuals and institutions to advance their own selfish agendas. Through a process known as the "Hegelian Dialectic" the American people have been tricked into demanding the wrong economic reforms. For the benefit of those who have not yet heard of the Hegelian Dialectic, let me briefly explain how it works. The Hegelian Dialectic is a 200 year-old, three-step process often used in "mass-brainwashing." Its formula is "thesis, antithesis and synthesis," and it was developed in the late 1700s by a German named George William Friedreich Hegel. The "thesis" portion of this formula represents a problem or crisis. In the case of these periods of great financial panics in American history, the thesis, which is the problem, was not only the panics, but public indifference, and/or ignorance, of the implementation of destructive monetary practices that allowed these disruptive financial panics to materialize. The "antithesis" is the opposite of the problem, or in the case of these periods of economic distress; the antithesis is a greater concern and public outcry for some kind of monetary reform. This is what those who have historically worked to exploit the American people and transfer our wealth unto them selves really wanted. Gary Allen, in his book, *"The Rockefeller File,"* indicates how public outcry enables the money masters to implement "synthesis." In this case, at the culmination of these periods of panics, synthesis is the policies that they wanted all along, nothing short of supplanting the duly elected government with what Congressman Wright Patman described as *"an independent, uncontrolled and uncoordinated government in the Federal Reserve System, operating the money powers which are reserved to Congress by the constitution."* Very few politicians understand the science of money, and they too are duped into accepting harmful monetary policy. Add to that, the propensity for the corporate-controlled media to label anyone that criticizes privately owned central banks and calls for them to be abolished, as a conspiracy theorizing nut, and our once economically sovereign democracy is subdued without firing a shot.

But thank heaven there have been a few wise and brave men in our government, who placed themselves at great risk to fight this beast. Some have even endured great loss to defend the spirit of the Constitution and our economic sovereignty. After the Panic of 1907, the Hegelian Dialectic was beginning to work as Americans cried out for monetary reform. Thomas J. Clark's book, *"The True American Way,"* recounts the efforts of one member of Congress, Rep. Charles A. Lindberg, who opposing privately owned central banks, put it all on the line and warned not only the unwitting citizens, but the other brave opponents of the bankers' plans: *"Those not favorable to the money trust could be squeezed out of business and the people frightened into demanding changes in the banking and currency laws which the money trust would frame."* The monetary scientists used economic booms and busts from the time of the passage of the National Banking Act of 1863 until 1913 to convince the American people that these economic problems were caused because America did not have a central bank. What America ended up getting was The Federal Reserve System.

In the final act, setting the stage for the Federal Reserve, J. P. Morgan and his associates crashed the stock market in 1907 then offered to prop up the American economy with money he created out of nothing with the blessing of Congress. G. Edward Griffin, tells us that Woodrow Wilson praised the success of Morgan pulling America out of the Panic of 1907 saying: *"All of this trouble could be averted if we appointed a committee of six or seven public-spirited men like J. P. Morgan to handle the affairs of our country."* The 1907 panic was the third worst stock market crash in U.S. history. To assuage the angry market and cover its losses, the government sold $36 million in bonds (remember, that's a lot of money by the standards of those days). The Crash started on January 19, 1906 with the Dow at 75.45, and didn't end until November 15, 1907, with the Dow ending up at 38.83. That's a total of 665 days of consistent losses in the neighborhood of -48.5%. Can you imagine the despair and desperation that plagued the consciousness of Americans who were forced into watching their savings, investments, businesses, and quality of life evaporate for almost two years straight?

The Hegelian Dialectic was within a hair's breadth of paying off. The monetary panics of 1879 and 1897 were nowhere near as severe as the panic of 1907. The 1907 panic required the government to intervene in what had previously been left to Wall Street to handle. All the hard work of the Money Trust was about to pay off; the time had finally come wherein they could eliminate the last vestiges of uncoordinated competition from wildcat banks. The government was taking a serious look at the Money Trust's plan to establish a central banking system that would be able to provide capital to all the nation's banks in a more coordinated way to insure that all the banks would be insulated from insolvency due to panic runs. And such a daunting task was simply too big to be left to the ad hoc regulatory dynamics of Wall Street. Gabriel Kolko explains the situation in his classic book, **"The Triumph of Conservatism:"** *"The crisis of 1907, on the other hand, found the combined banking structure of New York inadequate to meet the challenge, and chastened by any obstreperous financial powers who thought they might build their fortunes independently of the entire banking community ... The nation had grown too large, banking had become too complex. Wall Street, humbled and almost alone, turned from its own resources to the national government."*

The Aldrich Bill

The weakness of Wall Street being revealed prompted the government into accepting the Aldrich Vreeland Emergency Currency Bill. This bill allowed the National Banks to issue emergency fiat currency to help banks settle their reserve shortages due to the 1907 panic runs on the banks. This action opened the door for a bill creating the National Monetary Commission in 1908. Some people in the country knew that this proposed commission would be stacked with plutocrats, and would even likely be chaired by one of the biggest banker cronies in government—Sen. Nelson Aldrich.

Eustace Mullins, in his book, *"The Secrets of the Federal Reserve,"* said: *"A study of the panics of 1873, 1893, and 1907 indicates that these panics were the result of the international bankers' operations in London. The public was demanding in 1908 that Congress enact legislation to prevent the recurrence of artificially induced money panics. Such monetary reform now seemed inevitable. It was to head off and control such reform that the National Monetary Commission had been set up with Nelson Aldrich at its head, since he was the majority leader of the Senate."* The fact that Nelson Aldrich was working for the narrow interests of the international bankers, which constituted a threat to American economic sovereignty, was recorded in **Harper's Weekly,** May 7, 1910: *"A great many hundred thousand persons are firmly of the opinion that Mr. Aldrich sums up in his personality as the greatest and most sinister menace to the popular welfare of the United States ... What the south visits on the Negro in a political way, Aldrich would mete out to the mudsills of the north, if he could devise a safe and practical way to accomplish it."*

In preparation to perform their task, the National Monetary Commission spent two years in Europe studying the British banking model. But when they returned, no records or minutes were ever presented, and the sole tangible result of the commission's $300,000 expenditure was thirty volumes of books on European banking. Its only meeting was a secret conference held at Jekyll Island, which was never mentioned in the commission's publications. In his book, **"The Federal Reserve Act, Its Origins and Purposes,"** J. Laughlin said: *"The group interested in the purposes of the National Monetary Commission met at Jekyll Island for about 2 weeks in December 1910, and concentrated on the preparation of a bill to be presented to Congress by the National Monetary Commission. That bill was called the Aldrich Bill. In reality, the National Monetary Commission planned to assassinate the*

American economy and capture its wealth, transferring it into their private coffers." It should be noted that the Aldrich Bill was an official part of the Republican Party's platform.

After the Aldrich bill was introduced in Congress, Congressman Charles Lindbergh, in testimony before the Rules Committee on December 15, 1911, had this frantic warning: *"Our financial system is a false one and a huge burden on the people ... I have alleged that there is a Money Trust ... The Aldrich plan is the Wall Street plan. It is a broad challenge to the government by the Money Trust. It means another panic, if necessary, to intimidate the people. Aldrich, paid by the government to represent the people, proposes a plan for the trusts instead. It was a very clever move that the National Monetary Commission was created ... Wall Street knew the American people were demanding a .remedy against the recurrence of such a ridiculously unnatural condition. Most Senators and Representatives fell into the Wall Street trap and passed the Aldrich Vreeland Emergency Currency Bill. But the real purpose was to get a monetary commission which would frame a proposition for amendments to our currency and banking laws which would suit the Money Trust. The interests are now busy everywhere educating the people in favor of the Aldrich plan. Wall Street speculation brought on the Panic of 1907. The depositors' funds were loaned to gamblers and anybody the Money Trust wanted to favor. Then when the depositors wanted their money, the banks did not have it. That made the panic."*

The bankers went on to establish the National Citizens League. Under the careful guidance of Paul Warburg, the organization disseminated hundreds of thousands of educational pamphlets, organized letter-writing campaigns to Congressmen, supplied quotable press releases to the news media and used every other means at their disposal to create the façade of popular support for the Jekyll Island plan. Just as Lindbergh warned, the print media, which was largely controlled by Aldrich, went to work propagandizing the American people. The people were being told that the Aldrich plan would bring an end to monopolies, reduce the burden of government, and make financial panics disappear forever. But history has recorded that all of that was a well crafted lie by the most powerful money cartel on earth. The American people have historically been easily and adversely manipulated in this way.

A cartel is a group of independent businesses joined together to coordinate the production, pricing, or marketing of their members, thereby increasing profits and reducing competition. In this way, they force the public to pay higher prices for goods, products and services. We don't have to look in the past to find examples of how a cartel can use its power to mold popular sentiment for political leverage, there are examples occurring in our day. Example: On April 19, 2004, the media focused on Bob Woodward's book, *"Plan of Attack,"* with its revelations of the Saudi-controlled OPEC cartel allegedly engaging in price fixing of oil to ensure a Bush win in the 2004 presidential election. If this is true, then this revelation of George W. Bush making a deal with Saudi Arabia to lower fuel prices before the coming November election would give a vulnerable and unaware public, a perception of a *"strong economy."*

What the banking cartel that created the Federal Reserve hoped to accomplish with their Aldrich plan, was to gather all of the benefits to themselves that their self-serving apparatus could orchestrate, while keeping the pretense of benevolence toward a "strong economy." They wanted to keep the money supply disconnected from gold, which would establish for them the legal grounds to make our money supply more plentiful or elastic. This would allow the easy financing of various international, national and private ventures and the associated collection of interest on money they could create out of nothing. The main challenges that faced the Aldrich Bill were:

1) To keep control of the nation's money supply among them selves and end the competition for smaller rival banks.

2) To make the money supply more plentiful to recapture the industrial loan market.

3) To coordinate loan to deposit ratios of all the nations banks and consolidate them into one reserve to avoid currency drains (currency drains are the demand of money by other banks rather than depositors) and bank runs (demand of money by a large number of depositors at the same time).

4) To get the taxpayers to cover the losses in the event of a collapse of the banking system.

To convince Congress and the public that their findings were in the public's best interest the Jekyll Island strategists laid down the following plan of action:

1) Trick the public into believing the bank was a part of the government; don't even call it a central bank.

2) Form regional branches to create the appearance of nullified Wall Street control.

3) Begin with fair banking principles, and then quietly alter the objectives in favor of the money trust.

4) Utilize the Panic of 1907 to coerce national support for sweeping new monetary reform policies.

5) Offer the Jekyll Island plan as a solution to the problems of currency drains and panic runs on the banks.

6) Get universities to endorse the plan.

7) Finally, in what was perhaps the slickest move of all, the bankers themselves would have to denounce the plan to trick the public into believing that Wall Street was not in favor of it.

Now we must examine the Congressional opposition to the Aldrich Bill, and the bankers' clever and successful counter-measure—insuring their goal of creating another blood sucking privately owned central bank. I only hope that someday we will become proactive enough to heed the warnings of men like Congressman Lindbergh and like-minded patriots before the money-powers repo our country.

The Pujo Committee

The members of the Money Trust knew that Sen. Nelson Aldrich was a well known friend of big business and banking. They were also fully aware that any banking bill named after Aldrich was an easy target for the opposition. In spite of the egotistical Aldrich really wanting his name on the bill, this was all a maneuver to counter the moves of the opposition. They wanted the public to think that the Aldrich plan was the Wall Street plan, when in fact, it was only a decoy. To fool the public also into believing that Congress was looking out for the people, the Money Trust then stacked a committee in Congress with their agents to offer a new money policy that would counter the Aldrich Bill. Their agents in Congress formed a subcommittee of the House Committee on

Banking and Currency, headed by one of their best agents, Arsene Pujo of Louisiana.

Pujo practiced law in Louisiana before serving from 1903 to 1913 as a Democratic Congressman in the U.S. House of Representatives. From 1908 to 1912 he was a member of the National Monetary Commission, and he was definitely no friend to the economic welfare of the American people. In *"The Creature from Jekyll Island,"* G. Edward Griffin said: *"In 1913, the year that the Federal Reserve Act became law, a subcommittee of the House Committee on Currency and Banking, under the chairmanship of Arsene Pujo of Louisiana, completed its investigation into the concentration of financial power in the United States. Pujo was considered to be a spokesman for the oil interests, part of the very group under investigation, and did everything possible to sabotage the hearings ... The public was given the impression that Congress was really prying the lid off scandal and corruption, but the reality was more like a fireside chat between old friends."*

Having read many of the transcripts and commentaries on both of these hearings, I don't know which one was the most bogus Congressional investigation of the 20th century: the Pujo Committee, or the Warren Commission investigation into the assassination of JFK. Although the Pujo Committee's findings were a harsh indictment of Wall Street, there were many important questions that were never asked of the bankers who gave testimony. It was more of an indictment of the system, rather than an investigation into criminal activities of the bankers themselves. The combination of the Pujo Committee, and the help of Princeton, Harvard and the University of Chicago in propagandizing the public into believing that the Aldrich Bill was a Wall Street Bill, was an absolute brilliant move on behalf of the Money Trust. They were using the critics' warning against the critics themselves, and by doing so they turned their first plan into a decoy, and the public bought it. They scared the public into believing in their new plan, which appeared as a federal solution to Aldrich's bill that favored the bankers. The new bill was called the Federal Reserve Act. All that was needed now was a U.S. President in whom they could be sure the final Bill would be signed into law.

That president was Woodrow Wilson. In a book called *"The Federal Reserve Bank"* by H.S. Kennan, the author recalls that: *"Woodrow Wilson, President of Princeton University, was the first prominent educator to speak in favor of the Aldrich Plan, a gesture which immediately brought him the governorship of New Jersey and later the Presidency of the United States. During the Panic of 1907, Wilson declared that, 'all this trouble could be averted if we appointed a committee of six or seven public spirited men like J.P. Morgan to handle the affairs of our country.'"*

The Presidential Election Rigging of 1912 and 2000

The right to vote, and the entire voting process, is the central most defining aspect of the American democracy. It is a right that some of America's citizens in history were not allowed to have. Women were not allowed to vote until the early 20th century. It wasn't until the later half of the 20th century that black people were allowed to vote. Any attempts by black people at voting prior to that period resulted in their incarceration or worse.

The spirit of our democracy requires that every vote is important, and that every vote should be counted. It also requires that the right to vote by any and all eligible voters should be held as sacred and protected at all costs by the government. But as the citizens of the state of Florida and the nation found out when the closest election in U.S. history had to be decided by a Supreme Court ruling, effectively selecting George W. Bush as the winner of the 2000 Presidential race, elections can be flawed or compromised.

There were many people in Florida that claimed they were not allowed to vote, under what they cited as very dubious circumstances, even though they were registered and eligible to do so. There were massive recounts in Broward County, over the now infamous "hanging, dimpled, and pregnant chads" on the paper punch ballots. In a state wherein its electoral votes would decide who would be the next president of the United States, only 527 votes separated the two candidates. The election can only be described as a debacle which foreshadows future compromises to blood-won civil rights. In a May 17, 2004 article entitled "Vanishing Votes" by American Journalist Greg Palast, in *"The Guardian,"* Britain's premier Sunday newspaper, Greg's shocking comments are as follows: *"On October 29, 2002, George W. Bush signed the Help America Vote Act (HAVA). Hidden behind its apple-pie-and-motherhood name lies a nasty civil rights time bomb.*

"First, the purges. In the months leading up to the November 2000 presidential election, Florida Secretary of State Katherine Harris, in coordination with Governor Jeb Bush, ordered local election supervisors to purge 57,700 voters from the registries, supposedly ex-cons not allowed to vote in Florida. At least 90.2 percent of those on this 'scrub' list, targeted to lose their civil rights, are innocent. Notably, more than half—about 54 percent—are black or Hispanic. You can argue all night about the number ultimately purged, but there's no argument that this electoral racial pogrom ordered by Jeb Bush's operatives gave the White House to his older

brother. *HAVA not only blesses such purges, it requires all fifty states to implement a similar search-and-destroy mission against vulnerable voters. Specifically, every state must, by the 2004 election, imitate Florida's system of computerizing voter files. The law then empowers fifty secretaries of state—fifty Katherine Harrises—to purge these lists of 'suspect' voters.*

"*The purge is back, big time. Following the disclosure in December 2000 of the black voter purge in Britain's Observer newspaper, NAACP lawyers sued the state. The civil rights group won a written promise from Governor Jeb and from Harris' successor to return wrongly scrubbed citizens to the voter rolls. According to records given to the courts by Choice-Point, the company that generated the computerized lists, the number of Floridians who were questionably tagged totals 91,000. Willie Steen is one of them. Recently, I caught up with Steen outside his office at a Tampa hospital. Steen's case was easy. You can't work in a hospital if you have a criminal record. (My copy of Harris' hit list includes an ex-con named O'Steen, close enough to cost Willie Steen his vote.) The NAACP held up Steen's case to the court as a prime example of the voter purge evil.*

"*The state admitted Steen's innocence. But a year after the NAACP won his case, Steen still couldn't register. Why was he still under suspicion? What do we know about this 'potential felon,' as Jeb called him? Steen, unlike our President, honorably served four years in the US military. There is, admittedly, a suspect mark on his record: Steen remains an African-American.*

"*If you're black, voting in America is a game of chance. First, there's the chance your registration card will simply be thrown out. Millions of minority citizens registered to vote using what are called motor-voter forms. And Republicans know it. You would not be surprised to learn that the Commission on Civil Rights found widespread failures to add these voters to the registers. My sources report piles of dust-covered applications stacked up in election offices.*

"Second, once registered, there's the chance you'll be named a felon. In Florida, besides those fake felons on Harris' scrub sheets, some 600,000 residents are legally barred from voting because they have a criminal record in the state. That's one state. In the entire nation 1.4 million black men with sentences served can't vote, 13 percent of the nation's black male population.

"At step three, the real gambling begins. The Voting Rights Act of 1965 guaranteed African-Americans the right to vote—but it did not guarantee the right to have their ballots counted. And in one in seven cases, they aren't. Take Gadsden County. Of Florida's sixty-seven counties, Gadsden has the highest proportion of black residents: 58 percent. It also has the highest 'spoilage' rate, that is, ballots tossed out on technicalities: one in eight votes cast but not counted. Next door to Gadsden is white-majority Leon County, where virtually every vote is counted (a spoilage rate of one in 500).

"How do votes spoil? Apparently, any old odd mark on a ballot will do it. In Gadsden, some voters wrote in Al Gore instead of checking his name. Their votes did not count. Harvard law professor Christopher Edley Jr., a member of the Commission on Civil Rights, didn't like the smell of all those spoiled ballots. He dug into the pile of tossed ballots and, deep in the commission's official findings, reported this: 14.4 percent of black votes—one in seven—were 'invalidated,' i.e., never counted. By contrast, only 1.6 percent of non-black voters' ballots were spoiled.

"Florida's electorate is 11 percent African-American. Florida refused to count 179,855 spoiled ballots. A little junior

high school algebra applied to commission numbers indicates that 54 percent, or 97,000, of the votes 'spoiled' were cast by black folk, of whom more than 90 percent chose Gore. The non-black vote divided about evenly between Gore and Bush. Therefore, had Harris allowed the counting of these ballots, Al Gore would have racked up a plurality of about 87,000 votes in Florida—162 times Bush's official margin of victory.

"That's Florida. Now let's talk about America. In the 2000 election, 1.9 million votes cast were never counted, spoiled for technical reasons, like writing in Gore's name, machine malfunctions and so on. The reasons for ballot rejection vary, but there's a suspicious shading to the ballots tossed into the dumpster. Edley's team of Harvard experts discovered that just as in Florida, the number of ballots spoiled was—county by county, precinct by precinct—in direct proportion to the local black voting population.

"Florida's racial profile mirrors the nation's—both in the percentage of voters who are black and the racial profile of the voters whose ballots don't count. 'In 2000, a black voter in Florida was ten times as likely to have their vote spoiled—not counted—as a white voter,' explains political scientist Philip Klinkner, co-author of Edley's Harvard report. 'National figures indicate that Florida is, surprisingly, typical. Given the proportion of nonwhite to white voters in America, then, it appears that about half of all ballots spoiled in the USA, as many as 1 million votes, were cast by nonwhite voters.

"So there you have it. In the last presidential election, approximately 1 million black and other minorities voted, and their ballots were thrown away. And they will be tossed again in November 2004, efficiently, by computer—because HAVA and other bogus reform measures, stressing reform through

complex computerization, do not address, and in fact worsen, the racial bias of the uncounted vote.

"One million votes will disappear in a puff of very black smoke. And when the smoke clears, the Bush clan will be warming their political careers in the light of the ballot bonfire. HAVA nice day."

In the fallout over the debacle, the president's brother and Governor of Florida, Jeb Bush, decided to suspend the Broward County Supervisor of Elections, Miriam Oliphant, and instituted a "touch screen computer voting system." Many concerned citizens are still complaining about the security and integrity of the new computer voting process, citing the possibility of hackers sabotaging the machines. Many Florida voters have requested that the new computer voting machines be modified to provide a printed copy of the voter's selections as a paper trail in case of a recount. The governor denied their requests. Never before, in the history of elections in Florida, were there so many people saying that their voting rights were violated. Today, there are still many people who believe that the presidential election of 2000 was rigged. For more information on the possible rigging of the 2000 election, visit www.gregpalast.com.

If the outcome of the 2000 Presidential race had been rigged, it would not be the first time that a presidential race in America was rigged. Rigging the presidential election of 1912 was the only way that the Money Trust was going to be assured beyond doubt that their new plan for America's fourth privately owned central bank would get signed into law.

The presidential election of 1912 started out with only two candidates running for president: the Democratic candidate Woodrow Wilson, and the Republican William Howard Taft.

But by the time of the election, there were three candidates running. William Howard Taft was the incumbent, and the Money Trust knew that he wouldn't sign the bill, even though he was a friend to big business. So they ran the oldest trick in the book. They decided to shift some votes from Taft by running the Republican, Teddy Roosevelt, as the "Bull Moose" (Progressive Party) candidate. It worked like a charm: splitting the vote, guaranteeing the White House to their hand-picked, hand-groomed puppet candidate, Woodrow Wilson. Along with diluting the Republican's electoral support base, the instigated backdrop of political chaos enveloping the Republican Party was too much; the elections of 1910 and 1912 belonged to the Democrats.

This should show you that political partisanship is unimportant to the Money Trust and that they could care less about whether a Republican or Democrat sits in the White House. In 2000, Bush ran as a Republican. In 1912, Wilson was a Democrat. Both of these men received the blessings of the Money Trust. The advent of the Bush administration commenced almost simultaneously with an international War on Terrorism. Wilson's presidency almost simultaneously began with his signing of the Federal Reserve Bill into law. In both instances the monetary costs to the public were extremely high.

In 1912, no one could ever dream that the Republican bankers were working feverishly behind the scenes to elect a Democrat to the White House, but they were. Woodrow Wilson was funded by J. P. Morgan and Company, Kuhn, Loeb & Company, and Paul Warburg/Jacob Schiff. Roosevelt was also funded by J. P. Morgan and Company through their newspaper propagandists, George W. Perkins and Frank Munsey. These two hatchet men jointly contributed millions to facilitate Taft's political extermination. In a book called, *"America's Sixty Families,"* by Ferdinand Lundberg, the roles of Perkins,

Munsey, and the Money Trust in general are confirmed: *"In view of the vast sums of money spent by him [Frank Munsey] and Perkins, [Two Roosevelt supporters, both of whom were closely allied with the J. P. Morgan interests] to forward the Progressive campaign (of Roosevelt) and ensure Taft's defeat, the suspicion seems justified that the two were not overly anxious to have Roosevelt win.*

"The notion that Perkins and Munsey may have wanted Wilson to win, or any Democratic candidate (other than William Jennings) Bryan, is partly substantiated by the fact that Perkins put a good deal of cash behind the Wilson campaign.

"In short, most of Roosevelt's campaign fund was supplied by the two J. P. Morgan hatchet men who were seeking Taft's scalp."

Within the firm of Kuhn, Loeb & Company Felix Warburg was openly backing Taft so that the public would think the Money Trust wanted Taft to win. The Warburg/Schiff faction was also joined by Rockefeller's National City Bank in backing Wilson. Wilson's national campaign vice chairman and future Secretary of the Treasury, William McAdoo, had this warning: *"The major contributions to any candidate's campaign fund are made by men with axes to grind and the campaign chest is the grindstone ... the fact is that there is a serious danger of this country becoming a Pluto-democracy; that is, a sham republic with a real government in the hands of a small clique of enormously wealthy men, who speak through their money, and whose influence, even today, radiates to every corner of the United States."* McAdoo opposed Senator Nelson W. Aldridge's proposed system of privatized banks under control of the banking industry and advocated instead a central bank operated out of the Treasury.

Woodrow Wilson and Colonel House

With Woodrow Wilson finally in the White House, it was time to move the Jekyll Island/Federal Reserve plan into its final phase. A new bill was needed which would fool the controlling Populist wing of the Democratic Congress, the opposition leader William Jennings Bryan, and at the same time retain the substance of the old Aldrich Bill. So the Money Trust assigned Colonel Edward Mandell House to the role of Chief Advisor to President Wilson.

As a member of the London Connection, Colonel House worked more than anyone to get the United States into WWI on England's side. With the influence of House on the President, the Money Trust secured the massive war loans to England and France for the Morgan conspirators. Colonel House literally moved into the White House, and became a constant guiding companion to President Wilson in all areas of policy favorable to the Money Trust. In the book, **"The Strangest Friendship in History: Woodrow Wilson and Colonel House,"** by George S. Viereck, an assessment of the political under boss of America was made; *"For six years two rooms were at his disposal in the North wing of the White House. In work and play their thoughts were one. House was the double of Wilson. It was House who made the slate for the cabinet, formulated the first policies of the administration and practically directed the foreign affairs of the United States. We had indeed two Presidents for one!"* In other words, Colonel House was a shadow president—the unseen guardian of the Federal Reserve bill, the eyes, ears and voice of international banking interests in London and the United States, and the key player, insuring the success of the money masters' alliance in Washington.

The lust for money has always led to such ignominious unions. Such was the case in Judah when King Asa robbed his own country of its gold as payment to form an alliance with Syria against Israel. (1Kings 15:16-22) Yahweh rebuked this union because Asa gave away his country's wealth instead of relying on divine help in the face of adversity. (2 Chron. 16:7-10)

On our federal buildings and our money, are inscribed the words, *"In God We Trust."* In reality, this is a joke in America. Our presidents have no choice but to hearken unto the voice of moneymen, through their agents like Colonel House, and not the voice of God, as they profess. If they do profess to seek divine help in carrying out the duties of the office of the president, they are labeled nuts. But whether a president is religious or not, he is sworn to uphold the U. S. Constitution. The apostle Peter summed up the hypocrisy of our leaders, when they sell us out to those who have historically oppressed and extorted us: *"While they promise them liberty, they themselves are the servants of corruption; for of whom a man is overcome, of the same he is brought in bondage."* *(2 Pet. 2:19)* The Messiah also condemned the Pharisees, driving them from the temple *(Matt 21:13),* and whipped them verbally for their secret alliance with money: *"Woe unto you, scribes and Pharisees, hypocrites! For ye make clean the outside of the cup and of the platter, but within they are full of EXTORTION and EXCESS."* *(Matt. 23:25)* Emphasis on extortion and excess is mine.

The Colonel Houses of history, ill-advising presidents, engendering war and death for millions, are a prime example of how unbridled avarice, germinating within the conscious-ness of bought-off statesmen, impoverishes and slaughters the economic soul of our nation.

The Glass-Owen Bill

America was about to see the fruition of the epic moment that those dishonest banking families, who have accrued untold wealth throughout the world's history, have used every possible means at their disposal to bring into materialization. The long awaited and nefarious plan to create the Federal Reserve, which would be America's fourth privately owned central banking cartel, set up for profit, was almost complete.

In 1912 the international bankers, working to get the world's ultimate banking scam through Congress, cleverly recruited the Democratic Chairman of the House Banking and Currency Committee, Congressman Carter Glass from Virginia. With Glass now one of their nefarious little poodles, his job was to publicly condemn the bankers' decoy bill in the Congress, which was the Aldrich plan, while at the same time resurrect it from the dead in a new disguise. Glass staged public hearings, which were essentially rigged to disallow Rep. Charles Lindberg, father of the famous aviator, and the rest of the opposition in Congress, a persuasive voice in debate. Glass was joined by Senator Robert L. Owen in sponsorship of what would be known as the Glass-Owen Bill. Owen was no stranger to the banking industry. He was an Oklahoma bank president and studied central banking first hand in Europe. The Glass-Owen bill was filled with alterable components, only taking on the appearance of compromise. In reality, it was the same old Aldrich bill but with enough alterations to fool the Populist Party opposition. Their goal was to get the bill passed and perfect it later.

The international bankers and their agents within the American government then silenced one of the main voices of opposition when they guaranteed William Jennings Bryan the office of Secretary of State in Woodrow Wilson's administration. Bryan should have counted himself lucky, because in the game of rule by the rich, the competition is only offered a few alternatives; you either allow them to buy you off, be politically beaten, or be assassinated. With Bryan bought-off, victory for the Money Trust was assured.

But not only did the Money Trust have to trick the people and the opposition in Congress, they had to either fool or railroad the smaller banks that were very leery of Wall Street centralization as well. Andrew Frame was a member of the Executive Committee of the American Bankers Association who testified before the U. S. House Banking and Currency Committee hearings on ratification of the proposed monetary bill. Frame represented a group of western bankers in opposition to the Aldrich plan. The Aldrich plan had already been unanimously approved by the ABA, so Chairman Carter Glass asked him: *"Why didn't the western bankers make themselves heard when the American Bankers Association gave its unqualified and, we are assured, unanimous approval of the scheme proposed by the National Monetary Commission?"* Andrew Frame responded: *"I'm glad you called my attention to that. When that monetary bill was given to the country, it was but a few days previous to the meeting of the American Bankers Association in New Orleans in 1911. There was not one banker in a hundred who had read that bill. We had twelve addresses in favor of it. General Hamby of Austin, Texas, wrote a letter to President Watts asking for a hearing against the bill. He did not get a very courteous answer. I refused to vote on it, and a great many other bankers did likewise ... They would not allow anyone on the program who did not favor the bill."*

The hearings did not assuage the anxiety of the nation's smaller bankers. Although Glass denounced the Aldrich plan, his money policy still allowed the creation of a privately owned central bank. In the final analysis, both Congress and the public had been fooled by the Glass-Owen Bill, and the bankers in opposition had been railroaded.

The Federal Reserve is Born

On December 22, 1913, all of the Senators, except three, had gone home for the Christmas holiday. Their fellow Senators failed to formally adjourn, leaving the floor open for business. By a unanimous vote of only three, the Federal Reserve Act was sneaked through the Senate after already passing in the House. The bill was signed into law the very next day by the hand-picked, hand-groomed, puppet for the Money Trust—President Woodrow Wilson. America now had its fourth privately owned central bank called the Federal Reserve. By giving the Federal Reserve the unconstitutional authority to issue money created out of nothing at all, and control the credit of the United States, it ultimately controls our economic destiny.

Now we must briefly examine what is the second most powerful tool to wage war on the middle class—the graduated income tax, and the Federal Reserves' collection agency, the IRS.

The Federal Income Tax

Why was a progressive income tax imposed on America? The answer is not what most Americans inductively believe. Most people believe that the federal income tax, that we all hate to pay, has always been around and that we need that revenue to run the government. That is simply not true. The federal income tax has not always been around, and neither was it created as a means to run the government. The fact of the matter is that after the Federal Reserve bill became the law of the land, the bankers had to trick Americans into believing that taxes on your income fund the government and not their inflationary scheme of creating money out of nothing.

There are all kinds of taxes in America: state tax, excise tax, sales tax, property tax, inheritance tax, but the bankers were creating the worst tax of all: inflation. The Money Trust knew that if the American people ever realized that the economic dynamics of having a private central bank like the Federal Reserve was creating a burdensome and perpetually expanding unseen tax to be borne by every American citizen, that both elected officials and the public would revolt. Therefore, public ignorance was vital to the success of their scheme. This is the first reason for the tax; if the government eliminated the income tax and simply opted to run the nation on monetized debt (monetized bonds or government issued fiat currency), the people might just wake up and understand that the Federal Reserve was the burdensome debt machine that it really is. The second reason for the tax was to provide the ruling class aristocracy and free market elitists a lethal weapon to be perpetually used against the politically deaf, dumb, and blind middle class.

One week prior to the passage of the Federal Reserve bill, Congress passed a bill legalizing a federal income tax as a means to guarantee the national debt, period. The bankers knew that they had to strip the states of any potential voice or power over national monetary policy. It would not be wise for the bankers to depend only on the states' contributions toward the national debt service. They knew that eventually state legislators would revolt and either refuse to pay or put pressure on the banks to keep a limit on the growth of the debt.

As I said, the federal income tax has not always been around, even though the bankers had tried to create one prior to 1913. In 1895, they tried to establish a similar federal income tax and the Supreme Court found an income tax at the federal level to be unconstitutional. So what did they do? They did not have enough time, and did not want to go through all of the hazards of tampering with the Supreme Court, but they had to get the income tax established or all of the work they had done in creating the Fed could be abolished in a popular revolt. Knowing this, Senator Nelson Aldrich hurried the 16th Amendment to the Constitution through Congress, establishing the income tax. But the 16th Amendment was never fully ratified, so our federal income tax is not only unconstitutional, but it was rammed down our throats in a vicious attempt to choke the life out of any potential thrust toward true prosperity, sovereignty, and independence by the American people.

In 1946 Beardsley Ruml, head of the Federal Reserve Bank of New York, said: *"Given control of central banking and an inconvertible currency (a currency not backed by gold), a sovereign national government is finally free. Money worries and needs no_longer levy taxes for the purpose of providing itself with revenue. All taxation, therefore, should be regarded from the point of view of social and economic consequence."* The Federal Reserve and the income tax form a misunderstood and dangerous tool for controlling the American people. They both facilitate the redistribution of wealth from one class of citizens to another. Ruml said: *"The second principle purpose of federal taxes is to attain more equality of wealth and of income than would result from economic forces working alone. The taxes which are effective for the purpose are the progressive individual income tax, the progressive estate tax, and the gift tax. What these taxes should be depends on public policy with respect to the redistribution of wealth and of income. These taxes should be defended and attacked in terms of their effect on the character of American life, not as revenue measures."*

Tony Brown brilliantly points out in his book, **"Empower the People,"** that a personal income tax is a part of Communist doctrine: *"The second plank of the Communist*

Manifesto calls for a heavy or graduated income tax. Prior to the passage of the 16th Amendment to the Constitution in 1913, taxes on income were illegal in the United States. Since the introduction of the personal income tax, the average American works almost seven months of each year just to pay taxes.

"*Marx knew that his plan for economic tyranny would not be easily accepted in a democracy. He therefore included in the Manifesto the insightful provision that the Illuminati Ten Commandments should be applied differently in different countries. In the United States, the Communist Manifesto's Plank 2—promoting a graduated income tax—and Plank 5—a central bank—were sold to the people as democratic institutions aimed at preventing economic chaos and financial panics, such as the one in 1907 that had been manufactured by Illuminati agenturs, two German immigrants, Joseph Stalin and Paul Warburg ... as the famous Marxist economist John Maynard Keynes put it, 'the best way to destroy the Capitalist system was to debauch the currency' ....*

"*Freemason Keynes explains in 'The Economic Consequences of the Peace' how ' debauching the currency'—creating inflation by printing new un-backed notes of debt—gradually reduces the standard of living by secretly confiscating the income of the citizens and transferring it to the owners of the central bank that does the confiscating.*"

Under the Law of Moses, all males 20 years of age and above were required to pay an atonement tax during the census, consisting of a half-shekel of gold for the service and maintenance of the tabernacle. (Ex. 30:16, Ex. 31:12-14) The tax became known as the temple tax, and became a corrupt form of usury and socio-political manipulation in Jerusalem during the time of the Messiah (Luke 16:13), who also paid this tax (Matt. 17:24) but became violently opposed to it.

(Matt. 21:12) There were other biblical times that unfair taxes were levied against the people (Gen. 47:13-26, 2 Kings 15:17-20), but the evolution of the temple tax illustrates how the Hebrew moneychangers, gaining a monopoly on the half-shekel of the sanctuary, correlate with the Federal Reserve, a private banking cartel, unlawfully gaining control of our currency. In both instances, unfair and oppressive usury was exacted by an avaricious den of thieves.

Don't feel bad, the average person in America today, both citizen and politician, is still not aware that our income tax is unconstitutional. It is my hope that after you read this book, you will spread the word.

Booms and Busts

One year after the Federal Reserve Bill became law, Rep. Charles Lindberg had this warning about the Fed's ability to create periods of economic booms or busts: *"To cause high prices, all the Federal Reserve Board will do will be to lower the rediscount rate ... producing an expansion of credit and a rising stock market; then when ... business men are adjusted to these conditions, it can check ... prosperity in mid-career by arbitrarily raising the rate of interest. It can cause the pendulum of rising and falling market to swing gently back and forth by slight changes in the discount rate, or cause violent fluctuations by a greater rate variation, and in either case, it will possess inside information as to financial conditions and advance knowledge of the upcoming change, either up or down. This is the strangest, most dangerous advantage ever placed in the hands of a special privilege class by any government that ever existed. The system is private, conducted for the sole purpose of obtaining the greatest possible profits from the use of other people's money. They know in advance when to create panics to their advantage. They also know when to stop panic. Inflation and deflation works equally well for them when they control finance."*

G. Edward Griffin, in *"The Creature from Jekyll Island,"* indicates between 1920 and 1929, a period of escalating booms and busts culminated with the greatest fleecing of the American people in U.S. history. The bankers had decided to do exactly as Rep. Lindberg had warned and crash the market, transferring over 40 billion dollars from the American people to their private coffers. A paraphrased version of Griffin's roaring 20s cycle is chronicled as follows:

Up: The Fed inflated the economy to pay for WWI, causing a rise in prices.
Down: In 1920, the Fed raised interest rates to tame inflation. Recession follows, wiping out small business and farms.
Up: In 1921 the Fed lowers interest rates to halt the recession and help European trade. The debt grew and so did inflation.
Down: In 1923 the Fed tightened interest rates to stop inflation.
Up: In 1924, the Fed lowered interest rates to banks, creating 500 million in new money, leading to wild speculation in the market and ultimately a rise in prices.
Down: The 1926 Florida land boom collapses, and the economy follows.
Up: In 1926, the Fed lowers interest rates again. Boom follows.
Down: In 1928, Fed raises rates to halt the boom.
Up: Fed institutes time deposits, requiring a smaller reserve ratio (percentage of bank assets upon which their loans are based). This offset the Fed's contraction of credit.
Up: Fed bails out the British pound, increasing our money supply by 2 billion dollars in 1928.
Down: In the summer of 1928 the Fed sold Treasury Bonds on the open market, raising interest rates, thus contracting the money supply.

Both stock market crashes—1929, where the Dow lost 89.2% of its value in 714 days, and 2000-03, where the Dow lost 77.8% of its value in 648 days—followed the end of these types of boom and bust cycles. Each time the public is fleeced in this way, insiders are warned in advance, when and how to get out of the market, making a fortune off of the destruction.

How the Fed's Money Machine Works

How does the Federal Reserve create money out of nothing? First, the Federal Reserve's Open Market Committee approves the purchase of U.S. Bonds (a government I.O.U.), or some other instrument of debt, using only electronic credits to the seller's bank. These credits are not based on real money; the Federal Reserve creates them as mere bookkeeping entries. Secondly, the banks then use these imaginary deposits as reserves against withdrawals. Then, the banks can loan out over ten times the amount of their imaginary reserves to new borrowers, with interest. In this way, a Fed purchase of 10 million in U.S. Bonds turns into 100 million dollars of newly created money. In other words, they loan out up to ten times the amount of money they actually have on reserve. Keep in mind, these reserves exist only as bookkeeping entries. There are no reserves containing anything of intrinsic value. This corrupt and inflationary practice is called fractional reserve banking. It expands our money supply. The reason why it is inflationary is that the more money we have in circulation, the less our money is worth. This is why the dollar will never buy what it used to.

To contract or reduce the money supply, the Fed then reverses the process. The Fed sells the bonds to the public. Money pours out of the purchaser's bank. Loans must be reduced by ten times the amount of the sale, in order not to deplete their imaginary reserve. Thus a sale of a 10 million-dollar bond by the Federal Reserve results in 100 million dollars being removed from the American economy.

This method of expansion and contraction of the money supply only benefits the stockholders of the Federal Reserve because it 1) creates misdirected meaningful bank reform, 2) prevents debt-free currency like President Lincoln's Greenbacks from returning, 3) grants bankers the right to arbitrarily create 90% of our money supply by using the dishonest fractional reserve principle, 4) grants centralized overall control of our nation's money supply to the jurisdiction of a few men, and 5) establishes a privately owned central bank with a high degree of independence from the government.

This kind of dishonest currency manipulation, found in Biblical times, is called inflation today. Moneyed vultures scientifically created it then, just as they do today. The prophet Amos said: *"Hear this, O ye that swallow up the needy, even to make the poor of the land to fail, saying, when will the new moon be gone, that we may sell corn? And the Sabbath, that we may set forth wheat, making the ephah small* [artificially reducing the value of that currency] *and the shekel great* [artificially increasing the value of that currency], *and falsifying the balances by deceit* [dishonestly manipulating money, and its exchange in their favor]? *That we may buy the poor for silver."* [institute debt slavery] (Amos 8:4-11) Thus we see that today's global debt slavery is not a new concept and practice. We must learn before it's too late, that throughout history no economy has supported and sustained its working class under this type of system.

Chapter Five

World War I

Sacrificing the Lusitania

*T*here seems to be no end to the lies that are told to the American people. From birth we are lied to—Santa Claus, the Easter Bunny, the Tooth Fairy, and the Boogie Man, to name just a few. I was always told that the reason World War I materialized was the assassination of the Austrian Archduke Francis Ferdinand. I was also taught that the U.S. entered World War I to defend democracy. But like the official versions of most other epic events in world history, both of these reasons simply do not illustrate the key answers to the question: why was America drawn into World War I? The real answer is, for the purpose of taking the American taxpayers for billions.

But money being the reason for war is nothing new. Since the advent of modern banking, war has been privately

113

owned central banks' most profitable business. Historically, the influence of these banks has directed the geo-political and geo-strategic complexion of the entire world, ultimately for their own gain. War is the greatest generator of debt on earth. As such, as long as we allow privately owned central banks to operate, then their poodles in government will always implement the type of deceptive foreign policy that ultimately leads to war.

Let's see how America's entry into World War I was really instigated. First of all, we need to ask what was the primary method used to finance the war? The answer is the government's war bonds, sold to the Federal Reserve, secured the money to purchase war materials from associates of J. P. Morgan. Next, we need to ask what event was the trigger mechanism that drew America into the war. The answer to that question is the sinking of the Lusitania.

The Lusitania was a British passenger ship owned by a competitor of the Morgan cartel, loaded with American passengers, departing from New York on May 1, 1915. This would be the kind of murderous act that the Money Trust knew would be enough to convince a reluctant American public to get involved in Europe's war. The attack on the Lusitania, sadly, was the perfect means to get America involved in World War I. America and England both knew that the Lusitania was a target because of the war materials she carried from America to England. The German embassy in Washington knew as well. They even filed a formal complaint to the U. S. government, charging it was violating international treaties of neutrality. America denied the charges. In the meantime England began to flounder.

The desperation that England felt, because of the awesome power of Germany's U-boats, was overwhelming.

The Germans sank more than 5,700 surface ships during the war; England was in peril. U. S. Treasury Secretary William McAdoo said: *"Across the sea came the dismay of the British—a dismay that carried a deepening note of disaster. There was a fear, and a well grounded one, that England might be starved into abject surrender ... On April 27, 1917, Ambassador Walter H. Page reported confidentially to the President, that food in the British Isles was not more than enough to feed the civilian population for 6 weeks to 2 months."*

The complications associated with shipping activity in Europe jeopardized J. P. Morgan's war bond market, which was the primary source of war funding. Add to that, the fact that investors stood to get clobbered if England lost the war, simply because there was no way that Germany would honor investment deals made to bring about its destruction. The bankers weren't about to let that happen. In the book, ***"Woodrow Wilson and World War I,"*** Robert Ferrell confirms the situation: *"In the mid thirties, a Senate Committee headed by Gerald P. Nye of North Dakota investigated the pre-1917 munitions trade and raised a possibility that the Wilson Administration went to war because American bankers needed to protect their allied loans."*

So without a doubt, the attack on the Lusitania was a setup. The ship, passengers, and crew were placed directly in harm's way by a man who America teaches today, was one of the greatest statesmen of all time—Winston Churchill. At that time, Churchill was Lord of the Admiralty for Great Britain. Using the power of that office in 1914, Winston Churchill ordered British ships to disregard German U-boat orders to halt and search merchant ships. He did this not simply because he knew the ships were carrying munitions and did not want it discovered; as I've already said, the German embassy was well aware of that fact. No, he ordered innocent people aboard the

Lusitania in defiance of this routine, but nervous verification procedure, to intentionally provoke German aggression. To further increase the likelihood of a German attack on innocent American passengers, Churchill ordered British ships to remove their names from their hulls.

Either these moves were the greatest military blunders in history, or as far as Britain's war position is concerned, and in spite of the costs to America, they were the greatest strategic moves in history. Churchill boasted about his cold-blooded strategy in a book called, *"The World Crisis."* *"There are many kinds of maneuvers in war ... There are maneuvers in time, in diplomacy, in mechanics, in psychology; all of which are removed from the battlefield, but react often decisively upon it ... The maneuver which brings an ally into the field is as serviceable as that which wins a great battle."* Colonel House was asked by the King of England, George V, *"What will America do if the Germans sink an ocean liner with American passengers on board?"* House responded, *"A flame of indignation would sweep America, which would in itself probably carry us into the war."*

On May 7, 1915, a German U-boat sank the Lusitania. 1,195 souls were lost, 195 of them were Americans. The cry for war had begun. Fed up and outraged, William Jennings Bryan resigned as Secretary of State. Bryan understood that America was being swept away by propaganda in the media generated by Wall Street and the newly created Federal Reserve.

Today we can read *"The Intimate Papers of Colonel House"* by Charles Seymour and discover that Colonel House sent two telegrams from England to President Wilson, urging him to enter the war: *"America has come to the parting of ways, when she must determine whether she stands for civilized or uncivilized warfare. We can no longer remain neutral spectators ... our position amongst nations is being assessed by mankind ... In the event of war, we should accelerate the manufacture of munitions to such an extent that we could supply not only ourselves but the Allies, and so quickly that the world would be astounded."* Congress was whipped into action by the Wall Street- controlled press and the president.

On April 16, 1917, America entered the war. After passing the "War Loan Act" on April 24, 1917, the bankers would get a whole lot richer from the interest they would collect when Congress committed to borrowing approximately 38 billion; nearly every dime was created out of nothing by the Federal Reserve. The Money Trust finally had what they wanted since 1887, the ability to harness all of the profit potential of a major war in Europe. After all, this is the main function of a private central bank—war funding.

Just as the current Bush administration does not hesitate to challenge the patriotism of any institution, politician, or citizen, that opposes the war in Iraq, Woodrow Wilson did the same thing. In an address to the nation on October 13, 1917, supporting centralization of banking power, and framed around war support, Wilson said: *"It is manifestly imperative that there should be a complete mobilization of the banking reserves of the United States. The burden and the privilege (of the allied loans) must be shared by every banking institution in the country. I believe that cooperation on the part of the banks is a patriotic duty at this time, and that membership in the Federal Reserve System is a distinct and significant evidence of patriotism."* An article entitled ***"Espionage History 1917-1918,"*** published by Page Wise, Inc., recalls the attempts of the Wilson administration to silence public criticism of the war through the passage of the Sedition Act of 1917 and the Espionage Act of 1917: *"Despite earlier widespread resistance to entering the war, once war was declared American society was overwhelmed by patriotic fervor, quickly rising to the level* *of wartime hysteria. Deliberately stirred up by an intense propaganda campaign to encourage enthusiasm for the war, this patriotic fervor soon developed into rigid ideological conformity and outright suppression of all forms of dissent. All progressive, dissident, socialist, radical, or pacifist groups became targets of repressive actions by the government, and often also by private vigilante groups ....*

"With enormous popular support, Congress passed the Espionage Act of 1917, prescribing fines of up to ten thousand dollars and prison sentences of up to twenty years for a whole list of vaguely defined antiwar activities. The Sedition Act of 1918 (also called the Sedition Amendment to the Espionage Act) was even more draconian, imposing heavy penalties on anyone convicted of using disloyal, profane, scurrilous, or abusive language about the Constitution, the government, the military, or the flag. Similar laws were passed in several states as well. Those who spoke or wrote against the war were arrested in droves. Over fifteen hundred people were charged under these laws for the crime of expressing an opinion the government did not agree with."

There must be a thin line between patriotism and stupidity, because in reality, America was fighting not only to subdue the axis powers, but also to subdue themselves under a crushing debt and inflation. The money supply doubled from 20 to 40 billion during the war, confiscating 50% of the American people's wealth through the invisible tax of inflation. Remember, the more money we have in circulation, the greater its value is depreciated.

Once again, the people had been robbed in this ancient partnership between the political and monetary scientists. Winston Churchill sought tactical military advantage, J. P. Morgan sought the tremendous profits of a world at war,

Colonel House wanted political power, and Woodrow Wilson wanted to gain unchallengeable political and strategic advantage in the post-war era League of Nations. Wake up, America, there are thieves in the temple, and they're doing it again.

The Bolshevik Revolution

As is the case with the American people's perspective on the origins of World War I, we have never been taught the real reasons for the Bolshevik Revolution. They taught us in school that the reason the people in Russia revolted against the Tsars was because they were fighting against the tyrannical oppression of Tsar Nicholas II, and for a fair and equitable distribution of resources. We never stopped to question how a people in such declared economic dire straits were able to fund such an insurrection. What were the forces that aided them in their quest for change? Where did the money come from to fund the necessary propaganda, weapons, and various other elements of that turbulent insurgency? Who stood to profit? What were the geo-strategic, geo-political, and above all, global economic dynamics and by-products of the Russian Revolution?

The Bolshevik Revolution in Russia was in reality a coup, financed by Wall Street. The planning, leadership, and especially the financing came not from Russia but from international financiers in Germany, Britain and America. In a book called, *"My Life,"* by Leon Trotsky, the man himself reveals to us the Wall Street role in the recruitment and financing of revolutionaries to topple the Tsar. In the book, Trotsky speaks of a wealthy benefactor he called "Dr. M." The identity of the mysterious Dr. M. is revealed to us as being none other than Jacob Schiff by G. Edward Griffin in *"The Creature from Jekyll Island."* Griffin said: *"It must have been a curious sight to see the family of the great socialist radical, defender of the working class, enemy of capitalism, enjoying the pleasures of tea rooms and chauffeurs, the very symbols of capitalist luxury. In any event it is now known that almost all of his (Trotsky's) expenses in New York, including the mass rallies, were paid for by Jacob Schiff."* It turns out that the revolutionaries in Russia were recruited by Jacob Schiff, head of Kuhn, Loeb & Company of New York. These revolutionaries were trained in New York to distribute propaganda, which Schiff paid for, to indoctrinate Russian dissidents into rebellion against their own government. Leon Trotsky was Schiff's chief revolutionary, conducting mass rallies in New York, which were all paid for by Schiff. When Trotsky was arrested as a German agent threatening England's war effort, President Woodrow Wilson ordered his release. As Antony Sutton said in his book, **"Wall Street and the Bolshevik Revolution"**: *"President Woodrow Wilson was the fairy godmother, who provided Trotsky with a passport to return to Russia to carry forward the revolution."*

But not to mention the role of John D. Rockefeller's Standard Oil of New Jersey, and his interest in global oil markets, would be a mistake. In 1863 J. D. Rockefeller only had one refinery. By 1872, Standard Oil controlled 25% of the American oil market, and by 1879 he dominated 95% of the U.S. market, and 90% of all oil exports. Rockefeller enjoyed a monopoly until Russia began drilling in the Great Baku fields on the Caspian Sea. With the financial backing of the Rothschild family, by 1888 Russia produced and sold more oil on an international scale than Rockefeller's Standard Oil. A. Ralph Epperson, in his book, **"The Unseen Hand,"** said: *"The Russian Revolution of 1917 came not at the end of a period of stagnation and decay, but rather after a period of more than a half century of the most rapid and comprehensive economic progress, and with this came the development of the middle class, the enemy of the conspiracy ... the Russian Revolution of*

1917 was in truth a revolution instigated by American and European oil interests to wrest control of the Russian oil fields from the Rothschild-Nobel combination." As far as the Rothschilds were concerned, knowing that the East/West oil conflict would eventually lead to war, it was in their best interest to create a worthy industrialized adversary to America and England for the purpose of future exploitation of both sides in preparation for war. This was the beginning of serious East vs. West geo-political conflicts of interest that would lead to the Cold War and its associated proxy wars.

But there were other influences that opened the door to revolution in Russia. Just as the Haitian victory over the French, the only nation in the west, besides the United States, that won their independence in a fight against their colonial oppressor, had great influence in inspiring slave uprisings and the Abolitionist movement in America, so did the French revolution influence Russia's revolution. George Katkov's book, ***"Russia 1917,"*** gives us the account of how Napoleon's defeat gave the Russian people a clear model to follow. The subsequent occupation by Russian troops and visiting Russian aristocracy was used as an occasion to broaden the hegemony of Russian secret societies. Katkov said: *"There is no doubt ... that a widespread net of conspiratorial organizations modeled after (French) freemasons' lodges worked for revolution in Russia and played a decisive role in the formation of the first provisional government."*

Fearing being targeted for the imposition of a privately owned central bank in their country, the Russian government offered aid to Lincoln during the Civil War. They knew if America fell to the international bankers, they would be next. The big banks never forgave Russia for its support of Lincoln and his Greenback policy. In fact, Russia was the last major European nation to refuse to accept a central bank. Three years after World War I began, the Tsar was finally toppled in Russia and socialism was instituted there. All this was accomplished by the international bankers.

Why finance communism? Gary Allen in his book, *"None Dare Call It Conspiracy,"* had this to say: *"If one understands that socialism is not a share the wealth program, but is in reality a method to consolidate and control the wealth, then the seeming paradox of super rich men promoting socialism becomes no paradox at all. Instead it becomes logical, even the PERFECT tool of power-seeking megalomaniacs. Communism, or more accurately, socialism, is not a movement of the downtrodden masses, but of the economic elite."* Congressman Louis McFadden said: *"The course of Russian history has indeed, been greatly affected by the operations of international financiers ... The Soviet Government has been given United States Treasury funds by the Federal Reserve Board acting through the Chase Bank. England has drawn money from us through the Federal Reserve banks and has re-loaned it at high rates of interest to the Soviet Government."*

During the Cold War years, most Americans had no idea how the Communist government of the U.S.S.R. came to power and was economically sustained. Our leaders have lied to us and taxed us immensely to build up our military forces against their contrived threats. The establishing of an East vs. West strategic paradigm, through the sinister machinations of the international bankers and their poodles in para-governmental organizations like the Council on Foreign Relations and the Trilateral Commission, created astronomical debt for both sides during the Cold War. We should all shudder when we remember how this same elitist inspired, banker-funded, corporate-exploited, Cold War nearly destroyed civilization during the Cuban Missile crisis. This is a reckless and dangerous game that we have unwittingly participated in. As Lenin explained his rationale for accepting Wall Street's terms: *"The capitalists of the world and their governments, in pursuit of conquest of the Soviet market, will close their eyes to the indicated higher reality and thus will turn into deaf, mute, blind men. They will extend credits, which will strengthen for us the Communist Party in their countries; and giving us the materials and technology we lack, they will restore our military industry, indispensable for our future victorious attack on our suppliers. In other words, they will labor for the preparation of their own suicide."*

Chapter Six

Para-Governmental Organizations

The Council on Foreign Relations

*T*he ultimate goal of the international bankers is total control of the wealth of the entire world. To begin coordinating this effort, Cecil Rhodes, who became fabulously wealthy by exploiting the people of South Africa, established the Round Table Group in England. This group was established in America in 1921 and is known today as the Council on Foreign Relations. In his book, *"Rule by Secrecy,"* Jim Marrs tells us of the early plans for globalization, which created the need for an organization like the CFR to coordinate and carry out the free market ideological ground work for the New World Order: *"The council began as an outgrowth of a series of meetings conducted during World War I. In 1917 in New York, Colonel Edward Mandell House, President Woodrow Wilson's confidential adviser, had gathered about one hundred prominent men to discuss the post war world. Dubbing* *themselves 'the inquiry,' they made plans for a peace settlement which eventually evolved into Wilson's 'Fourteen Points,' which he first presented to congress on January 8, 1918. They were globalist in nature, calling for the removal of 'all economic barriers between nations,' 'equality of trade conditions,' and a formation of 'a general association of nations.'* Dominated by the Rockefellers, the Council on Foreign Relations is the most powerful group in America today. All of the key positions in the American government, including the presidency, are held by its members. The Council on Foreign Relations, and its sister organization, the Trilateral Commission, created by former National Security advisor Zbigniew Brzezinski and David Rockefeller, have been very useful to the Money Trust.

Concerning the Council on Foreign Relations, G. Edward Griffin, in **"The Creature from Jekyll Island,"** said: *"Almost all of America's leadership has come from this small group. That includes our Presidents and his advisors, cabinet members, ambassadors, board members of the Federal Reserve System, directors of the largest banks and investment houses, presidents of universities, and heads of metropolitan newspapers, news services and TV networks. It's not an exaggeration to describe this group as the hidden government of the United States."*

The Council on Foreign Relations was established in Paris in 1919, along with its British counterpart, the Royal Institute of International Affairs. All of these groups are what I like to call, para-governmental organizations. Like the Federal Reserve, they have the appearance of government agencies, but they are not. Also like the Federal Reserve, they have as much or more influence as the duly elected government. They are in the business of controlling public opinion. Operating in secret, they use the likes and dislikes of the influential people that they surround, to manipulate them into acting in the best interest of their agendas.

Even though the CFR has only 3000 members, today they control over three-quarters of the wealth in America. Right now the State Department and the CIA are under the firm control of the CFR. Every Presidential Administration since Woodrow Wilson has been made up of hundreds of CFR members. They work together to use any means necessary to influence the President to act in the best interest of the CFR. When the agenda of the CFR is at odds with the public, the best interest of the American People is compromised.

Presidents Eisenhower, Ford, Carter, Bush, and Clinton have been members of the CFR. Every Supreme Court is dominated with CFR insiders. Justices Stephen Breyer, Ruth Bader Ginsberg, and Sandra Day O'Connor are CFR members. The CFR is the American counterpart of the Royal Institute of International Affairs in Great Britain. The members of these groups profit by creating tension and hate, instituted by those operating at the core. Their targets include British and American citizens. Those members on the periphery are, by and large, not privy to the agenda of the elite within the core. Like drones, they simply carry out their duties without the slightest inclination of the true and ultimate direction of CFR policy.

Gary Allen reveals in his book, *"None Dare Call It Conspiracy,"* that *"FDR once said: 'In politics, nothing happens by accident. If it happens, you can bet it was planned that way.'* To ensure that there are no accidents in the so-called evolution of democracy, the CFR created a group called "the Secret Team," to implement psycho-political operations. These dubious mass behavioral modification operations, coordinated by the CFR's "Special Group," evolved from the CFR Psychological Strategy Board (PSB).

In an article called *"Why Isn't the CFR in the History Book?"* the geocities website describes the mass psycho-manipulation apparatus operating within the CFR. It tells us

127

that the Psychological Strategy Board, established by President Harry S. Truman, was run by CFR members Gordon Gray and Henry Kissinger. Many of those operations were focused at Americans. So believe it or not, the very attitudes, perceptions, the political and sociological consensus of the American people are being psychologically manipulated. Have you ever heard the expression, "You can fool some of the people some of the time, but you can't fool all of the people all of the time?" It's true. Some very influential people were not fooled by the CFR's Psychological Strategy Board. Eisenhower was forced to act. He issued an executive order changing its name to the Operations Coordination Board (OCB), which remained under the control of Gray and Kissinger. In his crusade against America's out of control covert intelligence apparatus, President Kennedy abolished the OCB. It then became the "Special Group," which was not formed by Executive Order; therefore it cannot be abolished, and still exists today. Thus, unwarranted psychological influences upon the last bastion of freedom on earth, the individual's thoughts and will, remain compromised.

On September 12, 1939, CFR members Walter H. Mallory, Executive Director of the Council on Foreign Relations, and Hamilton F. Armstrong, Editor of Foreign Affairs, began to take over the State Department, forming groups of experts in all aspects of geo-politics. The project lasted until 1945 under the name of the "Council on Foreign Relations War and Peace Studies." Hamilton Fish Armstrong was its Executive Director, presiding over its 362 meetings from 1939 to 1945.

By February 1941, with the establishment of the "Division of Special Research" (DSR), the CFR infiltration of the State Department was complete. The DSR was set up to formulate economic, political, territorial, and national security international policy.

In 1942, the CFR people within the State Department created the "Advisory Committee on Postwar Foreign Policies." Under the leadership of its Chairman, Secretary Cordell Hull, its vice chairman, Under Secretary Sumner Wells, its Executive Officer, Dr. Leo Pasvolsky, who was also Director of the DSR, along with Hamilton F. Armstrong, James T. Shotwell, Isaiah Bowman, Norman H. Davis, and Benjamin V. Cohen, the geo-political policy of the CFR became the official policy of the U.S. State Department.

In 1944 members of the "Council on Foreign Relation's War and Peace Studies Political Group" were invited to be active members at the Dumbarton Oaks conference on world economic arrangements. In 1945 these men, along with members of Britain's "Royal Institute of International Affairs," were active at the San Francisco conference, which helped create the United Nations.

In 1947 a covert psychological operation forcing the Marshall Plan on the American public was implemented by the CFR. The so-called Marshall Plan expanded debt slavery through Europe, under the guise of post war reconstruction, development, and investment. The money that American-based multinational corporations made rebuilding Europe after World War II is staggering, and the CFR's psychological manipulations apparatus was fully implemented to ensure popular support.

In 1950 another CFR/State Department psycho-political operation created support for one of the most influential documents of the Cold War—NSC-68. The NSC (National Security Council-68) gave the role of world policeman to the United States for the purpose of halting the spread of Communism. This allowed broad expansion of the military industrial complex, and the largest military establishment in peace time history. Since the drafting of NSC-68, the National Security-related budget has skyrocketed from $22 billion in 1950, to over $400 billion in 2004, despite there being no more threat from the Soviet Union. Keep in mind, their national security programs bankrupted and destroyed the Soviet Union. And guess what—thanks to the secret efforts of some members of the Council on Foreign Relations and Bush's unprecedented unilateral war policy, we're next.

The intelligent question we should be asking, since America is broke, is where are we going to get the money to fund the NSC mandate? How much interest will we have to pay on the loans? What will happen if we have to default?

The Trilateral Commission

The Trilateral Commission was established in 1973, largely, but not exclusively, by the efforts of Zbigniew Brzezinski. David Rockefeller, chairman of the Rockefeller family-controlled Chase Manhattan Bank and King of his family's global corporate empire, was also a major component in its creation. It is said that after reading Zbigniew Brzezinski's book entitled *"Between Two Ages: America's role in the Technetronic Era,"* Rockefeller was impressed enough by Columbia University's Prof. Brzezinski, to consider him one of the America's brightest scholars, and introduced the former National Security Advisor's idea at a Bilderberg meeting in 1972.

The Bilderberg group, like the Trilateral Commission, is largely financed and controlled by Rockefeller related interests. It is made up of the who's who of NATO's elite. The main difference between the much older Bilderberg group and the Trilateral Commission is that the Trilateral Commission is open to non-NATO participation; specifically the Japanese ruling elite. It is the addition of Japan into the global policy-planning network of Western Europe and the United States, that the term "Trilateral" is used to describe this commission. Basically, the Bilderberg Group sits a little closer, than the Trilateral Commission does to the planners at the core in the development of the New World Order.

Brzezinski's book wakes us up to the chilling realization of the dollar's peril in the New World Order. On page 300, he says Americans can expect a new monetary system, wherein the dollar will be replaced, and a reduced standard of living to achieve it. He said: *"In the economic-technological field some international cooperation has already been achieved, but further progress will require greater American sacrifices. More intensive efforts to shape a new world monetary structure will have to be undertaken, with some consequent risk to the present relatively favorable American position."* Brzezinski proposed forging a vast trilateral alliance between North America, Western Europe and Japan. According to Brzezinski, sequential development in the modern world makes internationalism unavoidable; he said: *"the American system is compelled gradually to accommodate itself to this emerging international context, with the U.S. government called upon to negotiate, to guarantee, and, to some extent, to protect the various arrangements that have been contrived even by private business."* The question is whether or not one worldism is the providence of elitism or a natural by-product of economic evolutionary forces. Either way, for the Trilateral Commission to protect its interests as they relate to its stated objective, the U. S. government must submit to a scary new global recalibration. Brzezinski believed that the developed nations must produce political leaders who would ensure that America's geopolitical interests would be protected as much as possible in this global realignment. To put it in another way, because the international order of this emerging new economic environment, in its political, economic, and social construct, must inevitably exist within a paradigm controlled by the needs of multinational banks and corporations, Americans must accept the unavoidable pains of the birth and nurturing of neo-internationalism.

One of the commission's primary goals was to send a Trilateralist president to the White House in 1976. They chose the unknown Democratic Governor of Georgia; Jimmy Carter. According to David Horowitz, co-author of *"The Rockefellers: An American Dynasty,"* *"Atlanta is Rockefeller Center South."* The choice came down to either Jimmy Carter or Florida Governor Rubin Askew. Carter was chosen because of the trade relationship he established with Japan while Governor of Georgia; the man was a natural Trilateralist. Both men ran for President during the 1976 campaign, but Carter clearly had the stronger Rockefeller connection, and was favored by Brzezinski at the first Trilateral Commission meeting in Japan during the spring of 1975. The Trilateral Commission's skillful use and strong influence of the media helped to get the "populist" Carter elected. They simply framed his candidacy as the Washington outsider; clean and forthright, compared to old Tricky Dick Nixon and his pardoner Gerald Ford.

Jimmy Carter became America's first Trilateralist U.S. President. As a member of the Trilateral Commission, he would be able to implement many of their economic and strategic goals. It is interesting to note how the debt service of the Panamanian government was a major issue when President Carter gave away the Panama Canal. It is also sad to recall the hostage crisis, and how it would later help set the stage for the secret arms deals, covert drug running, and the other CIA black-ops, which were backdoored out of the Reagan/Bush White House. The American public came to know the culmination of these black-ops as the Iran/Contra scandal.

Again, the often unspoken, but I believe ever-present cold hard question in the hearts of many is, did these events materialize under of the providence of elitism or were they a natural by-product of economic and geopolitical evolutionary forces.

But before the hostage crisis, it appears that the Carter administration was compromised in a CIA black operation, sanctioned by the State Department under the auspices of National Security mandate, which worked to secretly and successfully overthrow the Shaw of Iran. A. Ralph Epperson's book *"The Unseen Hand"* recounts the memoirs of the Shaw himself when he said: *"The Americans wanted me out. Certainly this was what the human rights champion in the State Department wanted."* A newspaper report in the *"Arizona Daily Star"* dated September 12, 1980, on page 10A tells us one of the main reasons why the Carter administration wanted the Shaw out; the Shaw *"repeatedly argued in his memoirs that for years the great multinational oil companies, possibly in league with the U.S. government had been subverting his rule because of his insistence to get a greater share of oil revenues."* This is strange; I thought OPEC set oil prices, not big oil companies. To add a little credence to this assertion, a book called *"The Energy Cartel"* by Norman Medvin, describes the three major oil companies of Iran as joint ventures with U.S. oil companies. Medvin says that the **Iranian Offshore Petroleum Company** is a joint venture with **CFP, Atlantic Richfield, Cities Service, Kerr McGee, Sun, and the National Iranian Oil Co.** Medvin also identifies **The Iranian Oil Consortium** is a joint venture with **BP, Shell, Gulf, Mobile, Exxon, Texaco, Standard Oil of California, CFP, and Am. Independent.** Finally, Medvin indicates a joint venture between **Lavaan Petroleum Co.** and the interests of **Atlantic Richfield, Murphy Oil, Union Oil, and the Iranian Oil Co.** If Norman Medvin is correct, and these joint ventures were valid at that time, then it is not a stretch to believe that any Iranian momentum toward nationalizing their oil fields is a plausible motivation for a Coup to be implemented.

The bottom line is that organizations, like the Council on Foreign Relations, the Trilateral Commission, and the Bilderberg Group, by the mere shifting of the weight of their enormous influences, can sometimes dangerously compromise the will of the people, the will of Congress, and the Constitution of the United States. The havoc they sometimes inherently create around the world has been the prime cause of growing international anti-American sentiment. In a *"Time/Europe"* poll, 84% of over 300,000 Europeans believe that the United States is the greatest threat to world peace. It's something to think about.

Warren G. Harding

Americans were fed up with Woodrow Wilson. In fact, Woodrow Wilson was fed up with himself as well. Wilson would later regret signing the Federal Reserve Bill, saying: *"I am a most unhappy man. I have unwittingly ruined my country. A great industrial nation is controlled by its system of credit. Our system of credit is concentrated. The growth of the nation, therefore, and all our activities are in the hands of a few men. We have come to be one of the worst ruled, one of the most completely controlled and dominated Governments in the civilized world no longer a Government by free opinion, no longer a Government by conviction and the vote of the majority, but a Government by the opinion and duress of a small group of dominant men."* Later when referring to the Illuminati, Wilson was quoted as saying: *"There is a power so organized, so subtle, so complete, so pervasive, that they had better not speak above their breath when they speak in condemnation of it."*

From a visionary standpoint, Wilson's lament came too late; the establishment of the fourth privately owned central bank, the Federal Reserve, assured the loss of American economic sovereignty. The American people elected Warren G. Harding as President, who didn't approve of America's secret involvement with financing Bolshevism. During that time, there was an avalanche of gold into America from Europe. This helped the economy to boom during World War I; the roaring 20s were about to begin. The wartime economy allowed Harding to reduce America's war debts by 38%. Both Harding and his successor Calvin Coolidge reduced taxes, increased tariffs and reduced inflation. Two years after his election, Harding took sick and suddenly died in office. No autopsy was performed on his body.

Many historians have assessed Harding as an indecisive president, but his decisiveness toward the policies of the international bankers, probably cost him his life. He didn't approve of their oppressive policies and neither did the American people. Harding and his Secretary of State, Charles Evans Hughes, tried to reduce the taxpayer's burdens. Historians agree that Harding's most significant achievement was the establishment of international treaties limiting the production of war ships, creating huge losses for the international bankers. It was an assault on the men who were secretly financing Bolshevism. In the final analysis, even though Harding was a member of the KKK, I wish more politicians in Washington would adopt his opposition to Wall Street corruption.

All of this new prosperity in America was too much temptation for the bankers to resist. They decided to pull off the largest transfer of wealth in U.S. history by crashing the stock market. With market investments at an all time high, speculation on liberal commodities and stocks running rampant, and on top of all that record low interest rates, the Federal Reserve began to tighten the money supply for the final assault on America. The roaring 20s were about to come to an abrupt end.

In April of 1929, Paul Warburg sent a memo to all his friends, warning that a collapse of the economy was about to occur and to pull their money out of the stock market. All of America's financial giants made enormous profits during the crash. A. Ralph Epperson, in his book *"The Unseen Hand,"* said: *"One of those fortunate speculators who got out early was Bernard Baruch, the individual who brought Winston Churchill to witness the crash. He had said: 'I had begun to liquidate my stock holdings and to put my money into bonds and into a cash reserve. I also bought gold.'* Another who got out early was Joseph P. Kennedy, father of President John F. Kennedy, who in the winter of 1928-29 got out of the market. The profits he took from the sale of his holdings were not reinvested, but kept in cash. A significant portion of Joseph P. Kennedy's wealth was acquired at this time; not all of it was made bootlegging.

The robber barons of today, Ken Lay, Gary Winnick, Steve Case, and Charles Schwab, were able to pull off a repeat, in principle, of what happened in the 1920s, because most people today are indifferent and still don't understand the true economic dynamics of this plutocracy. Arianna Huffington, in her book *"Pigs at the Trough,"* gives us a great summary of the wanton disregard for the working class by today's robber barons, and the false notion of *"shared destiny"* in the 21st century free market. Arianna asks us: *"How can there be talk of a shared destiny in a nation where just over one percent of the population (170 billionaires, 25,000 deca-millionaires and 4.8 millionaires) control approximately 50% of the entire country's personal wealth? Where the richest 20% earn 48.5% of the income, and the poorest 20%, merely 5.2%? Where, since 1980, real income for the bottom fifth of families fell by $800, while for the top fifth, it rose by $56,800?"*

The Crash of 1929

We have arrived at the point in this book that reveals one of the greatest economic crimes in recorded history — the great stock market crash of 1929. Thinking that periods of economic upheaval have their genesis in the random forces of the market place, most people don't look at the stock market crash of 1929 as a crime, but it was.

Let's summarize the anatomy and the physiology of the crash. The infamous events are as follows. In the spring of 1928, the Federal Reserve began to arbitrarily raise interest rates, which severely contracted the money supply, choking off credit, bringing a decade of wild stock market speculation and investments to an abrupt end; the roaring 1920s were over.

By August 9, the Federal Reserve's easy credit policy was completely reversed and the discount rate (the amount of interest the Fed charges on loans made to other banks) skyrocketed. In both England and the United States, bank reserves naturally began to shrink and so did the money supply. In this way, massive amounts of money was taken out of circulation by the Fed, which caused the market to begin to slide on September 19, 1929 and continuing until October 29, when the exchanges were crushed by an avalanche of selling.

Within a single day, millions of investors were wiped out. Within 12 months over 40 billion dollars had been transferred from the investors and speculators to the hands of those insiders who were poised and set to take advantage of the crash. Suddenly, people who had become rich in the stock market went broke overnight. Many of these victims committed suicide because they were unable to cope with their sudden poverty and financial chaos. But the insiders had prior warning of the crash. On February 6, 1929, the Federal Reserve issued a warning to all of its members to get out of the stock market. The member banks then issued warnings to their list of preferred customers. In March of that same year, Paul Warburg's annual report to the stockholders of the

International Acceptance Bank issued this warning: *"If the orgies of unrestrained speculation are permitted to spread, the ultimate collapse is certain not only to affect the speculators themselves, but to bring about a general depression involving the entire country."*

At the same time, men like John D. Rockefeller, Paul Warburg, Bernard Baruch, Joseph P. Kennedy, and their fellow members of America's financial elite, vastly increased their fortunes by purchasing stocks at a fraction of their worth during the crash.

People scrambled to get their money out of the banks as the chaos and panic continued in the weeks following the crash. So great was this panic that President Roosevelt, in March of 1933, shut down the banks; declaring a banking holiday. This was done to keep banks from becoming insolvent. Remember, banks only keep a fraction of their deposits on hand to cover withdrawals. If too many people show up at the same time wanting their money, under the fractional reserve system, the banks cannot pay.

There is much more that can be said on the crash of 1929 but I think Louis McFadden summed it up best. On May 23, 1933, McFadden brought impeachment charges against the Federal Reserve Board for causing the stock market crash of 1929. He said: *"I charge them with having taken over 80 billion from the U. S. government in the year 1928 ... I charge them with having arbitrarily and unlawfully raised and lowered the rates on money, increased and diminished the volume of currency in circulation for the benefit of private interest."* As I have already said in this book, McFadden died mysteriously. But I neglected to add the fact that, before his death, there were two attempts by gunmen to assassinate him.

If an ordinary person were to become involved in the practice of lending money at interest, and then manipulating the rate of interest in order that he could obtain more and more of the borrowers' wealth, then suddenly restrict or stop lending anymore money once the borrower has become totally dependent on the lender, that lender would be arrested and sent to prison for racketeering.

The Aftermath

After the great stock market crash of 1929, America braced itself for the worst. The immediate effects of the crash were felt primarily by risky speculators and those whose primary wealth consisted of stocks and other paper securities. The average American was not affected immediately but would be severely affected during the great depression years immediately following the crash.

Because of sustained high interest rates, and other market restraints by the government, along with its desire to use the crash as a means to justify even more controls than before, the monetary and political scientists were able to further extend their power over the money supply. Their prolonged high interest rates and other restraints, which meant very little money in circulation, led to widespread bankruptcies, massive unemployment and the hopeless malaise of a severe economic depression for the next 10 years.

In the 1930s the Fed began to slowly relax interest rates, pumping tons of fresh money into the economy. A multitude of new programs were designed and created to increase wages, prop up failing companies, stimulate construction, rescue the failing banks and protect their depositors, and guarantee home and farm loans. All this was done to help America out of the depression. The measures were all a part of FDR's "New Deal" policies that swept him into office. In spite of all economic recovery measures the economy was no better off in 1939 than it was in 1930. It was not until the outbreak of World War II and the massive industrial preparation for war, which created millions of jobs, that the depression was finally brought to an end.

Although most Americans today are not aware that the stock market crash of 1929 and the great depression of the 1930s were in great part caused by the Federal Reserve, this is a well-known fact to most top economists. Alexander James, of the Portland IMC, gives us the account of a 1996 radio address, wherein the Nobel Prize-winning economist, Milton Friedman, said: *"The Federal Reserve definitely caused the Great Depression by contracting the amount of currency in circulation by one-third from 1929 to 1933."*

As I pointed out earlier in this book, the contraction of the money supply is likened unto the contraction or restriction of the blood flow in the body, which can cause a heart attack, or a stroke, or ultimately death. When the Federal Reserve constricts our money supply like they did in 1929, our economy also suffers a stroke, killing the prosperity of the average American. The Federal Reserve successfully pulled off the greatest transfer of wealth in the history of capitalism. This is what happens when we allow corrupt men to acquire unwarranted power over our money and its issuance. This typifies what happens when the guiding hand of God, whomever or whatever you know that to be, is restricted. I believe when we do not listen to the voice from heaven, or as Abraham Lincoln called it, *"the better angels of our nature,"* which means following the guiding voice within, speaking in righteousness, and we choose to follow corruption, we will experience a spiritual depression within the soul. I believe that this is why we have natural depressions; they reflect spiritual depressions. (Rom. 1:19-20)

Chapter Seven

World War II

Who Financed Hitler?

W orld War II lifted America out of the depression. But the cardinal point to consider is that a war of that magnitude requires powerful and well financed adversaries. So who financed Hitler? As Herbert Hoover and later Franklin Roosevelt were allegedly working to bring America out of the depression, billions of dollars were being spent by the United States rebuilding Germany after World War I. Rep. Louis McFadden, from the floor of Congress, warned that America was helping to bring Hitler to power 8 years before Hitler invaded Poland. He said: *"After W.W. I, Germany fell into the hands of the German International bankers. Those bankers own her lock, stock, and barrel. They have purchased her industries, they have mortgages on her soil, they control her production, they control her public utilities. The international bankers have subsidized the present government of*

141

Germany and have also supplied every dollar of the money Hitler has used in his lavish campaign to build up a threat to the government of Bruening. When Bruening fails to obey the orders of the German International bankers, Hitler is brought forth to scare the Germans into submission ... Through the Federal Reserve Board over 30 billion of American money has been pumped into Germany ... You have heard of the spending that has taken place in Germany ... modernistic dwellings, her great planetariums, her gymnasiums, her swimming pools, her fine public highways, her perfect factories. All this was done with our money. All this was given to Germany through the Federal Reserve Board. The Federal Reserve Board has pumped so many billions of dollars into Germany that they dare not mention the total."

After two assassination attempts, McFadden's heart failure and sudden death on Oct. 3, 1936, after a bout with intestinal flu, remains a mystery. ***"Pelley's Weekly"*** of Oct. 14 said: *"... Now that this sterling American patriot has made the Passing, it can be revealed that not long after his public utterance against the encroaching powers of Judah, it became known among his intimates that he had suffered two attacks against his life. The first attack came in the form of two revolver shots fired at him from ambush as he was alighting from a cab in front of one of the Capitol hotels. Fortunately both shots missed him, the bullets burying themselves in the structure of the cab ... He became violently ill after partaking of food at a political banquet at Washington. His life was only saved from what was subsequently announced as a poisoning by the presence of a physician friend at the banquet, who at once procured a stomach pump and subjected the Congressman to emergency treatment."*

In his book, ***"Trading With The Enemy (The Nazi-American Money Plot 1933-1949),"*** by Charles Higham, a

chilling indictment of various American international financiers' involvement in the clandestine financial backing of
Adolf Hitler's rise to power is revealed: *"It would be
comforting to believe that the financial establishment of the
United States and the leaders of American industry were united
in a common purpose following the day of infamy, the
Japanese attack on Pearl Harbor on December 7, 1941.
Certainly the American public was assured that big business
along with all of the officials of government ceased from the
moment the war began to have any dealings whatsoever with
the enemy. The assurance sustained the morale of millions of
Americans who bore arms in World War II and their kinfolk
who stayed at home and suffered the anguish of separation.
The heartbreaking truth is that a number of financial and
industrial figures of World War II and several members of the
government served the cause of money before the cause of
patriotism. While aiding the United States' war effort, they
also aided Nazi Germany's. From the beginning of Hitler's
rise to power, German industry was heavily financed by
American and British bankers. Declassified documents under
the Freedom of Information Act have revealed that most of the
largest U.S. corporations were knowingly invested in war
industries that were supplying the Nazis."*

Americans are unaware of who financed Hitler and how
it was done. Most of his power came from a chemical cartel
called I. G. Farben, which staffed Hitler's intelligence apparatus,
administrated his Nazi slave labor camps, and even hired John
D. Rockefeller's PR specialist, the New York public relations
firm of Ivy Lee, to help improve Hitler's public image in
America. Antony C. Sutton's book, **"Wall Street and the Rise
of Hitler,"** exposes the little known source of the enormous
economic power of I. G. Farben as none other than Wall Street
U. S. A. The author says: *"Without the capital supplied by*

Wall Street, there would have been no I. G. Farben in the first place and almost certainly no Adolf Hitler and World War II." Carroll Quigley's book, **"Tragedy and Hope,"** describes I. G. Farben as *"largely a J. P. Morgan production."* Ralph Epperson's book, **"The Unseen Hand,"** describes the initial organization of the Farben cartel: *"I. G. Farben had its beginning in 1924 when American banker Charles Dawes arranged a series of foreign loans totaling 800 million to consolidate gigantic chemical and steel combinations into cartels, one of which was I. G. Farben."*

Many of the brave men that fought the Second World War are still in a quandary over some of the tactical decisions regarding allied bombing raids over Germany. The few living veterans of World War II still can't figure out why factories and administrative buildings of I. G. Farben were spared upon instructions from the U. S. War Department.

The Nazi/American money plot included the Bank for International Settlements (BIS), based in Basel, Switzerland, which was Nazi-controlled but presided over by an American, Thomas H. McKittrick. The BIS was a joint creation of the world's privately owned central banks in 1930, including the Federal Reserve Bank of New York. The BIS was used as the primary depository of 378 million in gold. The problem with that is the gold had been looted from the national banks of Austria, Holland, Belgium, and Czechoslovakia. Some of the gold held at the BIS found its way there from Hitler's Reichsbank, where gold from the teeth fillings, spectacle frames, cigarette cases and wedding rings of murdered Jews was held.

Tony Brown's book, **"Empower the People,"** broadly illustrates the confiscation of not only Europe's gold but that of the United States as well: *"Anglophile conspirators were not* *satisfied with simply forcing the United States to abandon the gold standard for its currency; it wanted America's gold as well. In 1941, when we entered World War II, the U. S. owned nearly two-thirds of the world's good gold stock ... In 1945, 24 billion of good gold stock was at Fort Knox. By late 1959, twice the amount of U. S. gold reserves was found in Europe, by 1964 ... Fort Knox housed only 15 billion in gold."* Americans were forced to pay 55% of the total war effort on behalf of the allies, but along with America, every nation involved in World War II greatly multiplied their debt. The United States really took a beating; the debt exploded from 43 billion prior to the war in 1940 to almost 260 billion by 1950. Between 1940 and 1950 the Japanese people were hammered by an astronomical debt increase of 1350%. The French were not spared either, their debt increased by 583%, and Canadian debt increased by 417%. Even today, under the economic dynamics of a global war of terrorism, the game hasn't changed, the entire world is still addicted to money created out of nothing, and loaned out by the Federal Reserve.

World War II made billions for the international bankers who financed the participants on all sides, before, during, and after the war. It is amazing to understand that all that financing came from money created out of nothing at all by privately owned central banks like the Federal Reserve. Without privately owned central banks, the Second World War could not have fully materialized. If there is ever a World War III, which some say that the War on Terrorism is the Third World War, careful study will reveal that the Federal Reserve will be the most influential instrument of its instigators. Abolish the Fed now, before it is too late.

Roosevelt Calls in the Gold

Most Americans believe President Franklin D. Roosevelt was one of the best Presidents in American history. To quantify that view, Roosevelt's "New Deal" policies are credited for ending the depression, his handling of the war is also touted as superb and the fact that he was elected four times are all cited as quantifiable proof of true presidential greatness. But does that overall assessment take into account some of the compromises of the Roosevelt administration?

By way of executive order, President Franklin D. Roosevelt moved America a giant step closer in becoming a mere component in a One World government by debasing America's currency in a way similar to what the IMF and World Bank would do to Third World countries years later. In 1933, Roosevelt ordered all Americans to turn in their gold bullion and gold coins. Before that time, America's paper currency (Federal Reserve Notes), were fully backed by gold. In other words, a person could exchange paper money at the bank for a gold piece of equal value. At that time, written on Federal Reserve Notes was the phrase, *"Redeemable in lawful money."* After the 1933 gold confiscation, that phrase was removed and the notes only read, *"This note is legal tender for all debts, public and private."* From that moment on, America's currency was no longer based on gold, and became inconvertible or irredeemable paper. Americans were told that this had to be done to jump-start the economy during the depression. Refusal to comply resulted in $10,000 in fines, 10 years in prison, or both.

The irony in the situation is that Roosevelt was elected earlier on a gold-standard platform. Nevertheless, the American people's gold was called in at $20.67 per ounce. By 1935, when all the gold was safely tucked away in Fort Knox, the price of gold skyrocketed to $35.00 per ounce. Only foreigners were allowed to sell their gold at that price at that time. In other words, while Americans suffered and starved during the depression, America's financial rulers, having advanced warning and moving their gold out of America, could now sell it at a profit margin of 75%. This increase in the price of gold was not, and is not today, set by the free market. Twice daily in London, five of Britain's top dealers in bullion meet in the offices of N. M. Rothschild and Sons, and the City Bank, and set gold prices.

What the American people must understand is that these kinds of compromises to our economic prosperity are just as dangerous to our liberty as any weapon man has ever devised. As long as we continue to remain primarily concerned about our politically partisan, ethnic, and racial differences, and not be more concerned about who controls and manipulates our money, we will remain helpless to stop the death of America.

Chapter Eight

The International
Monetary Fund and the World Bank

*T*he carnage of Third World debt and its economic ripple is of epic significance. However, the consequences of its existence are perhaps the most misunderstood threat to the survival of our prosperity and liberty. Yet the average person in the United States does not understand that, from an economic perspective, the unaware citizens of the world's leading industrialized nations are indeed adversely affected in this process. Therefore it becomes expedient that we examine the direct concentrated creative forces, which spawn such dire economic maladies ravaging the Third World, preventing its prosperity, and causing depression and riots. Who or what malefic force controls their leaders, keeping them from being able to resuscitate their nations from economic asphyxiation?

When we examine the operation of the International Monetary Fund in the Third World, we will find its despotic fingerprints in a crime scene of epic proportion. Universal principles of justice have been broken in what can only be described as a calculated and historically incommensurable assault upon the weak by the strong. From the outset of the perilous debt crisis in 1982, those powerful U.S. and European financial interests behind the IMF have continued to bleed the Third World dry through the sullen art of usury.

If you or I had the same track record of managing a company the way that the IMF has managed the Third World's debt restructuring, there would be little doubt as to our termination. But because of the lack of accountability of a Board of Governors within the IMF, and like-minded men throughout history, implementing the plutocratic agenda of an ancient oligarchy, great crimes against every living thing upon the face of the earth continue. The destruction of social and economic institutions, environmental devastation, the illicit global drug trade, the international devaluation of currencies, poverty, famine, and war itself, are only a few of the aspects which are ultimately associated with policies of the IMF/World Bank controlled debt slavery of the Third World. They have had and continue to have a devastating ripple effect throughout the entire world.

Its modous operandi is the same as that of the Federal Reserve, but on a global scale. First they create money out of absolutely nothing at all, without the backing of gold, loan it out at interest to addicted governments, while at the same time gaining control of the political process. Then through imposing draconian stipulations for receiving these loans, the international bankers have assured the perpetuation of Third World debt slavery. These dynamics form the primary economic characterization of the New World Order.

Who established the
International Monetary Fund and Why?

In July 1944 at the Washington Hotel in Bretton Woods, New Hampshire, a meeting of the world's most prominent financiers, bankers, theoreticians, and politicians— all socialists—was held for the purpose of establishing what was to become the IMF. The two men who were at the helm of the meetings wherein the IMF was created were Harry Dexter White and John Maynard Keynes. Both of these men were Fabian Socialists, which is an ideology that I can't help but conclude as being dangerous to this nation. In his book, ***"The Economic Consequences of the Peace,"*** Keynes said: *"The decadent international but individualistic capitalism, in the hands of which we found ourselves after the war (W.W.I) is not a success. It is not intelligent; it is not beautiful; it is not just; it is not virtuous;—and it does not deliver the goods. In short, we dislike it and are beginning to despise it .... If you despise capitalism, and wish to replace the system with another that you prefer, it becomes imperative to find a way to destroy it. One of the most destructive methods of destruction is inflation, the debauching of the currency ... Lenin was certainly right."*

Subsequently it was proven that White was a member of a Communist spy ring, a fact known to be true and ignored by President Franklin D. Roosevelt. At which time, White, as Assistant Secretary of the Treasury, was also instrumental in causing the currency collapse of China by withholding all but 27 million in financial support during WWII. This comes in spite of the fact that in early 1945, Congress approved and allocated 750 million in allied wartime aid. In 1971, the U.S. Senate Committee on the Judiciary issued a 28 page document entitled ***"The Human Cost of Communism in China"*** in the ***"Review of the News,"*** February 23, 1972, which concluded

151

that China's revolution, brought on by currency collapse, was *"responsible for the deaths of as many as 64 million people."*

Now it must be noted that although the American people have been mis-educated and propagandized into believing that communism is a share the wealth system, it is in fact a transfer the wealth system, from the hands of the poor to the rich. We must understand the indisputable historical fact that the communist revolution in Russia was instigated, financed, and facilitated by banking interests in the United States. This was done for the purpose of establishing a East vs. West strategic paradigm, which would fuel their profits from the financing of a costly and economically oppressive Cold War. The astronomical costs of the Cold War, and its associated strategic proxy wars as its by-product, bankrupted the Soviet Union. It should be noted that the Soviet Union was one of two historically major obstacles to the New World Order, leaving only the U.S. and its Constitution as the sole remaining resistance. This is one reason the IMF was created—to supplant both sides in favor of a one world socialist order. This view is confirmed in **"The Creature from Jekyll Island,"** by G. Edward Griffin. He said: *"The 1944 meeting in Bretton Woods, New Hampshire, at which the world's most prominent socialists established the International Monetary Fund and the World Bank as mechanisms for eliminating gold from world finance; the hidden agenda behind the IMF/World Bank revealed as the building of world socialism."* The IMF/World Bank were created as international instruments of sovereign nationalistic destruction and the economic colonization of every nation on the face of the earth, thereby building the Fabian Socialist New World Order.

The Fabian Socialist doctrine, by which the IMF/World Bank operates, was first formulated by an elite group of intellectuals who formed a semi-secret society to advance their goal of world socialism. H. G. Wells regarded the early leaders of this group, George Bernard Shaw and Sidney and Beatrice Webb, as "the new Machiavellians." Their method for accomplishing this was the gradual dissolution of national borders through propaganda, legislation, guile, and deceit rendering all nations under one umbrella of economic exploitation. This philosophy guides international bankers today. It does not allow them to cultivate a sense of nationalism, patriotism, or humanism.

Once a nation has accepted the protocols of the New World Order and its system of privately owned central banks, they are enslaved by a global banking system, which disallows nationalistic economic sovereignty and the hope of financial freedom and prosperity. That nation's handpicked leader is either coerced or forced into pimping his country while his people starve. Take a look at Haiti, according to *"The Internationalist: Business Guide to the World—Mexico, Canada, and Latin America"* their reward for accepting the terms of the IMF is 80% unemployment, abject poverty 70%, and male life expectancy 49 years. Make no mistake about it, if the IMF is allowed to continue to create money out of nothing at all, loan it out at interest, get the dumbed-down citizens of America to co-sign these nefarious loans (without Congressional approval under the International Lending and Supervisory Act of 1983), our destruction is a foregone conclusion.

Structure of the IMF

Although it appears to be part of the United Nations, like its primary manipulator the Federal Reserve appears to be a part of the U.S. government, it too is not. The IMF and the World Bank are private and independent institutions. In fact the IMF was created one year before the UN was established in 1944.

A Board of Governors representing the world's privately owned central banks runs the IMF. It is funded by almost 200 member nations on a quota basis with the greater portion exacted from the world's 5 leading industrialized nations. Unfortunately for the taxpayers of America, the greater portion of that comes from the United States.

One of the main functions of the IMF is exchanging hyper-inflated and worthless currencies into dollars so those poorer nations can service their debt and facilitate transnational trade. The fact that their currencies have been rendered worthless, by reasons heavily associated with these 21st century moneychangers, only serves to magnify their debt burden and further facilitate the plunder of weaker nations. Now, far too much of their money has to be demanded for dollars in the exchange process. Remember, the book of Isaiah speaks about the devil weakening the nations. (Isa. 14:12)

End of the Gold Standard

Because of the elimination of the gold standard and the dubious implementation of the principle of fractional reserve banking (multiplying your and my deposits which are held on reserve by more than ten times), the IMF produces and lends its own intrinsically worthless money. Originally the IMF had to adopt the gold standard, but true to its Fabian creed, it never lost sight of its goal of a fait based (not backed by gold) international lending institution. As Keynes himself said in **"The Collected Writings of John Maynard Keynes Vol. V":** *"I felt that the leading central banks would never voluntarily relinquish the then existing forms of the gold standard; and I did not desire a catastrophe sufficiently violent to shake them off involuntarily. The only practical hope lay, therefore, in a gradual evolution in the forms of a managed world currency, taking the existing gold standard as a starting point."*

To facilitate the removal of the gold standard a new inconvertible (not redeemable in gold) monetary unit had to be created. So in 1970 the IMF introduced the SDR or Special Drawing Rights. Although these SDRs were described as "paper gold," there is no connection to gold or anything of intrinsic value. SDRs are another form of debt generating fiat money. In his book, *"When Your Bank Fails,"* Dennis Turner describes how SDRs work: *"SDRs are turned into loans to Third World nations by the creation of checking accounts in the commercial or central banks of the member nations in the name of the debtor governments. These bank accounts are created out of thin air. The IMF creates dollars, francs, pounds, or other hard currencies and gives them to a Third World dictator; with inflation resulting in the country where the currency originated ... Inflation is caused in the industrialized nations while wealth is transferred from the general public to the debtor country. And the debtor doesn't repay."*

The gold standard was finally killed on August 15, 1971 when President Richard M. Nixon issued an executive order, eliminating U.S. redemption of gold for its paper money. Since the dollar is the main currency used by the IMF, and before 1971 it was redeemable in gold at $35 per ounce, it established a limit on the amount of money the IMF could create. Therefore, thanks to Dick Nixon, the door is now wide open to worldwide debt-generating SDRs and further perpetual inflation within industrialized nations.

The oppression of trade imbalances

Trade imbalances occur when a nation's imports exceed its exports. Ultimately, no home, business, or government can continue to spend more than it earns. Sooner or later all methods of financing such debt will become exhausted and the debtor is bound to suffer great loss. The IMF's instigated destruction of domestic social, economic, and industrial infrastructure perpetuates the oppressive nature of trade imbalances. Thereby it chronically binds the heavy burdens of poverty, unemployment, illiteracy, homelessness, and disease upon less developed countries. You see, in order to receive loans to finance their trade deficits, Third World countries must submit to strict cuts in spending on health care, education, food subsidies.

Trade imbalances are financed by either borrowing, selling assets, or through the use of fiat money. Because politicians prefer borrowing to finance trade deficits, instead of open taxation, loans are issued and restructured over and over again by the IMF. The people guarantee these loans and are thereby taxed through the loss of land and natural resources in debt for equity swaps with the IMF. Selling assets, such as buildings, land, bonds, factories, and companies, are often used by governments to offset negative trade balances. However, we can now see how drastic sociological and political ramifications accompany foreign ownership and control over industry and commerce.

Currently the United States is the only country afforded the opportunity of financing its trade deficit with fiat money. Thus, while we get tangible goods and products from foreign countries, like China, who up until November 2002 enjoyed a 26 to 1 trade imbalance with America (for each dollar they spent with us we spent $26 with them), they got worthless paper money. Now under newly established World Trade Organization (WTO) compliance, China's trade imbalance will greatly contribute to the ultimate collapse of the U.S. job market, at the same time as their labor force is enslaved by western corporations. China and the WTO are helping to bring about the rapid de-industrialization of America. To make matters worse, the debt burden of China's corporations and their 80 percent default rate has forced them to sell their products at a loss. This is deflation, and it is spreading throughout the world and into America. It's going to be interesting watching our remaining anemic domestic corporations compete.

The American Dollar or Federal Reserve notes have not had the backing of gold at the IMF since 1971 but remain the standard by which all other currencies are measured. Even mentioning dollar devaluation by Greenspan as a possible method for balancing trade sends foreign governments running for cover. This is a part of the reason any U. S. stock market rally is unsustainable. As the dollar's value continues to collapse, foreign speculators will begin to sell their dollars for a more stable monetary unit, which is happening right now and creating millionaires in trading foreign currency. The result will be far greater difficulty financing our tremendous trade deficits with countries like China and massive inflation within the U.S. as the weakened dollar is dumped back into America and its purchasing power is destroyed.

Sociological and Political Ramifications of IMF/World Bank Policies

The perpetually expanding debt of Third World countries causes great hardship for their people. Their governments spend far more on debt service than on health care and education. This consigns millions of souls throughout less developed countries (LDCs) to hellish sociological ramifications, such as poverty, famine, disease (AIDS, Hepatitis, and Ebola), and ignorance. Therefore, no matter how much money is sent to starving children, solicited by a litany of TV fund raising efforts, the suffering and its ripple effect will continue until the debt slavery ends and the nations are allowed to develop and support themselves.

According to a 1996 UN study, examples in the area of child mortality rates (deaths per 1000 live births) in the Third World, as a result of IMF policies, are as follows: Niger 191, Angola 70, Zambia 112, Sierra Leone 164, D.R. Congo 128, Liberia 57, Malawi 137, Mali 134, Mozambique 133, Guinea-Bissau 132, Guinea 130, and UK US 6. It should also be recalled that the average life expectancy of a man in Haiti is only 49.33 years of age. One of the main reasons that these numbers are so astronomically high in LDCs is because they get ripped off so badly in the currency exchange process that they can never afford to acquire the outside materials necessary in building their nation.

Loans must always be repaid in **hard currencies** like the Euro, Japanese yen, Swiss franc, and the American dollar. The term hard currency is used because of its stability. LDCs have **soft currencies** because their value decreases as their debt rises, thereby requiring more of the LDCs' money to pay back the same amount in hard currency. For example, after World War II Germany would only agree to spend 3.5 percent of its export income on debt repayments. They argued that anything higher would be unsustainable. Today the world's creditor nations, including Germany, are demanding that LDCs spend as much as 75 percent of their export income on debt service. Could it be that this double standard in the structural adjustment of debt contains an element of racial nepotism? Could that, in part, explain why Mozambique now spends US $107 million every year servicing its debt? This translates into US $60 for every Mozambique man, woman, and child. In contrast, the country spends only US $2 per person per year on health and education. Could that be the reason for hopeless consignment of the people of Mozambique to abject poverty?

Take a look at Ghana. For each of her citizens, Ghana spends US $4 per year on health. In 1996 it spent US $26 on debt service. Do you really think they have a chance under that type of usury? Since 1990 Zambia has paid a total of US $4.8 billion in debt service, which is about one and a half times its total annual economic output.

The west expects debtor nations to pay even when loans were made to corrupt regimes, and even after new leaders are empowered, the people of the debtor nation have no voice in the matter. Such is the case in South Africa, Zaire, Cuba, and now Iraq. The suffering is further compounded when one considers the fact that these poorer countries cannot purchase industrial machinery for building roads, buildings, and cities. Nor can they purchase military hardware or any other vital big ticket items using their national currency. Sorry, Caterpillar and Lockheed/Martin will not take play money.

The citizens of Third World countries have also been made subject to personal dispossession. Literally, they are kicked out of their homes and off their lands, because IMF officials are guilty of giving state-owned companies, corrupt governments and developers the means to seize the lands of poor and illiterate peasant farmers, throwing them into an unstable and insecure future they are not prepared for. For example, a $530 million loan to India to start, expand or modernize two dozen open pit coal mines has started the expulsion of 10,000 adults from their lands and homes. Also critics charge that in Peru a World Bank-financed gold mine has not added nearly enough to the local economy to justify pushing poor farmers from their lands. Then there is the situation in Lesotho, where critics charge that the IMF/World Bank has not done enough to help those dispossessed by a series of dams.

It should be remembered that Thomas Jefferson said that by allowing private banks to issue a nation's currency and establish credit that banks *"will deprive the people of all property until their children wake-up homeless on the continent their fathers conquered."* This is now coming to pass because the IMF and the World Bank have become two instruments of national destruction. In an interview with Michael Chossudovsky, Professor of Economics at the University of Ottawa, by Jared Israel (4-16-00) see **emperors-clothes.com,** Professor Chossudovsky said: *"When the IMF goes into a country and requires the destruction of social and economic institutions as a condition for lending money—this is very similar to the destruction caused by NATO bombing. The IMF will order the closing down of hospitals, schools, and factories. That's of course more cost effective than bombing those hospitals, schools and factories, as they did in Yugoslavia, but the ultimate result is very similar: the destruction of the countries that accept the IMF. Like Bulgaria and Romania, they may not get bombed but they are destroyed with the pen."* In other words, war is, and as far as the slow painful gradualism of the Fabian turtle is concerned always has been, an obsolete means to an end, which is the destruction of national and political sovereignty and rebuilding a New World Order.

The Illicit Drug Trade and American Slavery

We cannot ignore the role of western monetary and political interventionism in the perpetuation of the international trade of illicit drugs, and the existence of drug lord gangsters in Third World countries. In Jared's interview with Chossudovsky this sullen issue is also candidly discussed. *"Chossudovsky: The military industrial complex, the intelligence apparatus and links to organized crime including the use of narcotics to finance conflicts are aimed at opening nations to Western control. Let's say you install Hacim Thaci (leader of the Kosovo Liberation Army) in the seat of government in Kosovo. It's much more convenient to have a gangster like this running a country than to have an elected Prime Minister that is responsible to citizens.* " In many cases, Third World countries like Colombia are forced into the drug business so that the proceeds in part may be used to service their debt to the IMF/World Bank.

No one can argue the point that the proliferation of illegal drugs in America has and continues to have a devastating affect. The drug trade is a vital component of global 21st century slavery, just as it was a vital component in pre-20th century American slavery. At that terrible time in our country, the British East India Company, based in Europe, financed the building of slave ships and their expeditions into Africa to bring slaves to market in America. These slaves then picked cotton, which was sent to England where peasants turned the cotton into cloth. The cloth was then traded for opium in India. The opium was then sold to the Chinese, and part of the proceeds were used to continue financing the slave trade, while the lion's share went into the coffers of the illuminati aristocracy who controlled the British East India Company. Today, it is the heirs of that aristocracy and their nefarious poodles in government, who have used every tool at their disposal, including the drug trade, and continue to enslave and inebriate every living thing on this planet.

The Washington Consensus

Now we must examine the Three Pillars of the Washington Consensus as issued through the IMF/World Bank from the outset of the debt crisis in the early 1980s to the present. We will start with **fiscal austerity,** which is strict fiscal discipline and restrictions in spending (especially on

socioeconomic programs, such as food subsidies, health care, and education) imposed on debtor nations. This first pillar of the Washington consensus has historically been a major cause of the perpetuation of poverty in developing nations. Joseph Stiglitz, former Chairman of President Clinton's Council of Economic Advisors and chief economist for the World Bank, as well as winner of the 2001 Nobel Prize in Economics, in his book ***"Globalization and its Discontents"*** said: *"While it is true that sustained reductions in poverty cannot be attained without robust economic growth, the converse is not true: growth need not benefit all. It is not true that a rising tide lifts all boats. Sometimes a quickly rising tide, especially when accompanied by a storm, dashes weaker boats against the shore, smashing them to smithereens. Understanding choices requires understanding the causes and nature of poverty. It is not that the poor are lazy; they often work harder, with longer hours, than those who are far better off. Many are caught in a series of vicious spirals: lack of food leads to ill health, which limits their earning ability, leading to still poorer health. Barely surviving, they cannot send their children to school, and without an education, their children are condemned to a life of poverty. Poverty is passed along from one generation to another. Poor farmers cannot afford to pay the money for fertilizers and high-yielding seeds that would increase their productivity. They are buffeted by forces beyond their control."*
I applaud Mr. Stiglitz for telling the truth, and I strongly encourage you to get his book. It is rare that ranking members of these international lending institutions will be as candid about the negative aspects of the Washington Consensus, and when they are, we should pay attention.

The second part of the Washington consensus is **privatization.** This requirement involves converting government-run industries into private ones. The Washington Consensus says that debtor governments must reduce their size and scope, so that more revenue is marked for debt service. The problem with this prescription is that private interests are always profit-motivated, usually corrupt, and often without regard for humanism, nationalism, or compassion for the poor.

What makes privatization so harsh is the fact that the pace of privatization is not in line with a sequence that is prudent or sufficient enough to provide macroeconomic (aggregate) stability. In other words, the pace and sequence of privatization simply does not regard nor allow enough time for safety nets to be implemented which would provide assistance for the loss of jobs and dispossession accompanied by corporate downsizing and streamlining. Therefore any resulting economic growth is almost always dual in nature; the rich get richer and the poor get poorer. Joseph Stiglitz had this to say: *"It is important to restructure state enterprises, and privatization is often an effective way to do so. But moving people from low-productivity jobs in state enterprises to unemployment does not increase a country's income, and it certainly does not increase the welfare of the workers. The moral is a simple one, and one to which I shall return repeatedly: Privatization needs to be a part of a more comprehensive program, which entails creating jobs in tandem with the inevitable job destruction that privatization often entails. Macroeconomic policies, including low interest rates, that help create jobs, have to be put in place. Timing and sequencing is everything."*

The Three Perils of Economic Liberalization

Now that we have focused on the first two pillars of the Washington consensus, fiscal austerity and privatization, we will now examine various aspects of **economic liberalization,** which is the third and final significant aspect of the Washington consensus. It is commonly agreed, even at the

IMF, that liberalization has been improperly prescribed and implemented. They have also admitted that capital and financial market liberalization contributed to the global financial crises of the 1990s, wreaking havoc on developing countries and rippling into the industrialized nations. Just as in privatization, all aspects of liberalization are imposed by the IMF as a condition for assistance. Again, the exacerbating factor is that all this is done at a reckless pace and sequence. What this means for the working class in America is higher unemployment as the few remaining U.S. based corporations move their manufacturing, assembling, and technical operations overseas, leaving only their administrative operations in America.

Trade liberalization by the IMF has been ordered faster than even that which is prescribed by the World Trade Organization, and has had a devastating effect on developing nations. The consensus in Washington often charges and convicts poor countries with anti-liberal trade practices, and forces one-sided trade agreements with those nations which do not have the means to defend themselves. Trade liberalization tied to high interest rates makes it more difficult for local businesses to access capital needed to expand or provide jobs for those who have lost their jobs when western companies move in, downsize, and streamline former nationally run industries. The ultimate result is job destruction and unemployment. In this way the U.S. Treasury department, banks, and corporations benefit by the realization of vastly disproportional gains. Nations such as China, which was forced into full WTO compliance in November 2002, has had to open up to many aspects of trade liberalization, albeit at a pace and sequence more sympathetic than that which is prescribed for most developing nations, but will still lead to total destruction of both its economy and more immediately ours.

In an article by the *"Global Policy Forum,"* entitled **"Economic Liberalization and Integration"** it is said that:

"Advances in communication and transportation technology, combined with free-market ideology, have given goods, services, and capital unprecedented mobility. Northern countries want to open world markets to their goods and capital and take advantage of abundant, cheap labor in the South, a policy often supported by Southern elites. They use international financial institutions and regional trade agreements to compel poor countries to "integrate" by reducing tariffs, privatizing state enterprises, and relaxing environmental and labor standards. The results have enlarged profits for investors but offered pittances to laborers, provoking a strong backlash from civil society."

It doesn't take a Nostradamus to envision a day in the near future when Anglo-America will have to demand some form of international affirmative action. In fact, people of all races, all throughout the Americas, are waking up and beginning to voice serious concerns about the dangers within our hemispheric economic model. Recently we saw protests again in Miami at the Free Trade Area of the Americas summit. The FTAA is basically an expansion of the North American Free Trade Agreement (NAFTA), requiring even more liberalization within the Third World. Those who protest these accords point to the fact that since NAFTA has been enacted most of the Third World has experienced a reduction on pre-capita income and gross domestic product. In the past, trade ministers and international banking officials have tried to blame the rise in popular protest to their agenda as a reason for the failure of their policies. But in an article by David Moberg on the **"In These Times"** website, that assertion is refuted: *"... trade ministers will not be able to blame the protestors alone for their likely failure in negotiating the FTAA. Opposition in Latin America is widespread; hemispheric governments disagree over what should be in the agreement, and more and more economists are recognizing that the model for economic development embodied in FTAA is deeply flawed."*

Again, back to China, whose ascension to the WTO is being called the greatest coming-out party in the history of capitalism; the U.S. Treasury Department, which is the largest IMF shareholder, has also pushed for faster **financial market liberation**. The reason for this, again, was well stated by Joseph Stiglitz, in his book, ***"Globalization and its Discontents,"*** when he said: *"This American demand for liberalization of financial markets in China would not help secure global economic stability. It was made to serve the narrow interests of the financial community in the U.S., which the Treasury Department vigorously represents. It was important that Wall Street get in, establish a strong toehold, before others. While the more advanced industrialized countries, with their sophisticated institutions, were learning the hard lessons of financial deregulation, the IMF was carrying this Reagan-Thatcher message to the developing countries, countries which were particularly ill-equipped to manage what was proven, under the best of circumstances, to be a difficult task fraught with risks."* Thus we see that financial market liberalization without an appropriate regulatory structure brings on total macro (aggregate) economic instability and often leads to rising interest rates.

As bad as trade and financial market liberalization were for developing nations, premature and rapid **capital market liberalization** was worse. Capital market liberalization involves deregulating the flow of stateless capital (private foreign investment money) in and out of the country. When short-term loans, contracts, and market investments come into a country and the recipient nation experiences down-turns in its markets, when the value of its currency plummets as exchange rates skyrocket, then loans are not restructured, contracts are not renewed, and stateless capital flees. This is a recipe for divestment and economic collapse. But the IMF evidently ignores or does not understand the volatility of these problems and continues to prescribe this highly destabilizing medicine for fledgling nations. And as always, the costs of the instability are disproportionately saddled upon the poor. Add to that, the fact that in many developing nations, most of the available wealth and resources are dominated by an ethnic minority, and it's easy to understand how the plight of the poor becomes that much more oppressive.

In her best selling book, *"World on Fire,"* Amy Chua brilliantly points out the chaotic dynamics of minority groups within Third World countries controlling most of the wealth and resources. Identifying groups like the Chinese in Southeast Asia, Jews in Russia, whites in Zimbabwe and Indians in East Africa and Fiji, Chua calls these groups "market-dominant minorities." Socio-economic stratifications within these societies result on the basis of the influence of these "market-dominant minorities." When these nations are dominated by market-dominant minorities, economic liberalization can have an extremely volatile effect. Chua argues that the pace of the introduction of economic liberalization and democracy into countries with market-dominant minorities is so great, that the two forces inevitably conflict with each other. She said: *"Markets concentrate enormous wealth in the hands of an outside minority, fomenting ethnic envy and hatred among often chronically poor majorities. Introducing democracy in these circumstances does not transform voters into open-minded co-citizens in a national community. Rather, the competition for votes fosters the emergence of demagogues who scapegoat the resented minority and foment active ethno-nationalist movements demanding that the country's wealth and identity be reclaimed by the true owners of the nation."* In other words, because a perpetual state of poverty is sustained only upon the majority ethnic group by forces emanating from within and from without of these developing nations, there is created a greater propensity for ruthless despotic leaders to rise from the ranks of the disenfranchised masses.

ANDRE MICHAEL EGGELLETION

The Political By-Product of
Economic Liberalization in Haiti

Nowhere in the world is the dynamic that Chua describes more boldly brought into materialization in these present times than in the Haitian political crisis of 2004. It is a classic case of how a perpetual state of poverty is sustained only upon the majority ethnic group by forces emanating from within and from without of a Third World nation. Whether by accident or intent, it is the economic policies inside and outside of Haiti that are creating the necessary breeding ground for ruthless despotic rebellious opposition to democracy to have risen from the ranks of the disenfranchised masses. The Haitian people have become so politically disoriented by poverty, hopelessness and starvation, that a small faction within the emaciated majority has chosen to shoot the government out of office, rather than vote it out of office.

Haiti has been the victim of a 200 year long U.S. policy of diplomatic isolationism. They cannot establish the necessary trade and diplomatic relationships with the rest of the world because of an American-led policy to intentionally isolate them on an international scale. Washington and Europe have chosen to allow the perpetuation of a failed state in this hemisphere to send a message to all imperial and colonial subjects of Anglo-imperialism; don't mess with us.

It all started in 1804, when Haiti became the only other nation in the western hemisphere, besides the United States, to win their independence in armed insurrection. When Haiti defeated the mighty French army, and expelled their French colonizers from the island, European aristocrats lost their colonial investments, which constituted a deeper and more intolerable dilemma. I can't tell you the shock waves that went through the American and European aristocratic society, because some rag-tag nation of Negroes had defied and overturned their colonial dominance. America feared that its slaves and their abolitionist benefactors would try to emulate Haiti's defiance, while England feared uprisings in Jamaica. Europe and America simply could not allow this rebellious momentum to stand; it was a threat to their hegemony. This is why Washington will never allow Haiti to develop a self-sustaining socio-economic infrastructure, or to have a sympathetic immigration policy with America; we are sending our imperial subjects a clear message.

But as a consequence in Haiti, as Amy Chua points out, the have-nots blame the haves for their plight. They blame the upper class in Haiti for the 78% unemployment, and 75% of the population being forced to live in abject poverty. Their response is a misguided and blind reactionary rage. The most recent violent protest and insurrection was orchestrated by the despotic rebel leader Guy Philippe, with the covert militaristic assistance of the CIA, against the democratically elected leader of Haiti—Jean Bertrand Aristide.

In the final analysis, in spite of the cries from CARECOM (the Caribbean community of nations) for a sympathetic and meaningful policy of engagement toward Haiti, Washington sabotaged a democracy in peril, implementing a policy of confrontation toward Aristide for not following the Washington consensus, and for seeking reparations from France. I describe what took place in Haiti as a low-intensity coup d'état, or a coup by proxy. We would rather destroy our country through catastrophic deficits trying to impose democracy halfway around the world in Iraq, than to support the notion of democracy just 600 miles away in Haiti.

Sadly this Washington Consensus has been the economic policy imposed upon almost every nation on earth. It has been the direct cause of the financial crises in East Asia, throughout the entire Pacific Rim of nations, Africa, South and

Central America, the Middle East, and Russia. This largely secret backdoor policy of the monetary scientists in the west, which is called the Washington Consensus, has helped to strategically destabilize the world and is a continuing factor behind global discontent, leaving some to conclude that terrorism is their only resort.

Cultural Diffusion in Western Civilization

To understand and appreciate how the monetary scientists' fundamental control over the nations of the world has been accomplished and maintained, we must first understand the basic historical aspects of the cultural diffusion of material and non-material elements of the core society toward the peripheral societies in western civilization. Professor Carroll Quigley, mentor to Bill Clinton and author of the 1300-page classic book on the evolution of the world's power structure, *"Tragedy and Hope,"* said: *"The powers of financial capitalism had a far-reaching plan, nothing less than to create a world system of financial control in private hands able to dominate the political system of each country and the economy of the world as a whole."* He exposes how control of the sequence, pace, and diffusion of cultural aspects of civilization, which are created at it's core, are carried outwardly to the peripheral areas in such a way which ensures that the core always exploits, controls, enslaves, and thereby devastates the peripheral areas. Concerning this fact he said: *"Many of the problems which the world faced at the middle of the 20th century were rooted in the fact that these different aspects of the European way of life spread outward into the non-European world at such different speeds that the non-European world obtained them in an entirely different order from that in which Europe had obtained them. In Europe the Industrial Revolution generally took place before the*

Transportation Revolution, but in the non-European world this sequence was reversed. This means that Europe was able to produce its own iron, steel, and copper to build its own railroads and telegraph wires, but the non-European world could construct these things only by obtaining the necessary industrial materials from Europe and thus becoming the debtor of Europe." He goes on to point out how virtually every aspect of the development of civilization is carried out in this way.

Now we can see that the architects of the New World Order are simply implementing this same pattern of conquest, using the world's financial institutions as the means to control the sequencing, pace, and diffusion of economic elements, designed to weaken the nations. Remember, Isaiah 14:12 reveals to us that the Devil would *"weaken the nations,"* and Proverbs 22:7 says that *"the rich ruleth over the poor and the borrower is servant to the lender."* If this is true, and I believe it is, then we are all slaves in a system which is evolving and growing more pervasive throughout the world. Thousands of books have been written which have warned us of this fact. Those who have exposed the system have done so at great peril. Anonymity is the most guarded tool of these money-changers and history has shown that they will stop at nothing to keep it.

The evolution of this ancient financial system, built upon usury and debauchery of currency, has brought us a world financial system today which is so pervasive that blaming any one organization or person for its perpetuation is ludicrous. The system is likened unto an out of control rampaging beast. Could this be what the apostle John described in the 13th and 18th chapters of the book of Revelations?

Just as diffusion of the unique and exclusive religious and non-material aspects of ancient Israel has inadvertently created a chaotic and divided ecclesiastical system in peripheral societies, which has often led to the spiritual impoverishment of many, it is the same principle of diffusion of material and non-material elements of western society that has impoverished the developing world. It is my contention that the architects of this economic system, beginning in ancient times, those in our day, and all who have endeavored to harness and perpetuates its usurious methodology throughout the ages, do the bidding of evil intentionally. Their deeds will ultimately lead to their own destruction. As Lenin explained his rationale for accepting Wall Street's terms: *"The capitalists of the world and their governments, in pursuit of conquest of the Soviet market, will close their eyes to the indicated higher reality and thus will turn into deaf, mute, blind men. They will extend credits, which will strengthen for us the Communist Party in their countries; and giving us the materials and technology we lack, they will restore our military industry, indispensable for our future victorious attack on our suppliers. In other words, they will labor for the preparation of their own Suicide."*

Chapter Nine

The Central Banking
Crisis of Global Stateless
Capital and the Crash of 1987

"And he causeth all, both small and great, rich and poor, bond and free, to receive a mark in their right hand and their foreheads: And that no man might buy or sell, save he that had the mark, or the name of the beast, or the number of his name." (Rev. 13:16-17)

*W*hen we examine the Federal Reserve System and its role in the later half of the 20th Century, we find that it is now impossible to blame any exclusive group or institution for the perpetuation of the current economic problems of the world today. The institutionalized debt of America today, which is five times greater than the debt in 1950, has grown to 7.2 trillion dollars, and is actually owed by we the people. Yes, to a large extent, we owe it to ourselves. How can that be, one might ask? The answer is simple. Congress does not live within its' means. To run the government, Congress has created 28% of the national debt by borrowing from the Social Security Fund, using government IOUs as collateral. Foreign investors own 27%, domestic private investors own the largest share totaling 37%. The Federal Reserve today only holds 8% of the national debt.

Could we actually be living in the system described by the Apostle John in the book of Revelations, wherein the aspects of the system which he describes in Rev. 18th Chapter, represents our current economic system? Maybe the mark of the Beast that John describes in Revelations 13:18 is not a physical mark on the skin. Nor, perhaps is it a computer purchasing and identification chip implanted beneath our skin, as many have imagined. It must be noted that the dictionary defines the word mark as: *"to distinguish; set off; characterize; as great scientific discoveries marked the 19th century."* When taken in this context, it isn't a stretch to say that our current economic system might be a manifestation of the great whore and the beast that John described, and those who promote it without regard for its oppressive aspects have indeed received its mark. They are marked by greed and unbridled avarice. In this context, the mark in the head is actually one's consciousness, which has been marked with the pursuit of materialism. The mark in the right hand is one's activity, marked by the actions striving toward satisfying materialistic desires. As well, our being victimized by taxation and inflation, which drives us so hard to earn a living that we loose sight of anything else, has become our mark. We cannot buy. We cannot sell. We cannot exist outside of this economic system. The number 666 or 6 in Hebrew theology represents or indicates the flesh, not only the physical flesh, but fleshly concepts, imaginations, and opinions. The Federal Reserve and the economic system it has spawned are based on the fleshly principles of greed and power, not the righteous principles of fairness and justice. The system itself is the beast.

Seeing that history is a great teacher, it would not be prudent to ignore the role of the Rothschilds, the Schiffs, the Morgans, the Rockefellers and the wealthy banking families which set up the current economic system. We must, however, understand that central banking in America is now over 200 years old and deeply entrenched in our society. No longer dependent on the clever devices of any one individual or family, these banks have gained the illusion of respectability. The American people have staked their hard-earned savings into the corporations and stock market which has grown up around these banks. Therefore today the allegations of reform minded politicians, which were once railed against the exclusivity of Wall Street and its' disconnection with Main Street, laying the blame at the feet of the super rich, no longer totally apply. Daniel Gross in his book *"Bull Run,"* said: *"In 2000, when we speak about the ownership of companies, we are no longer exclusively talking about the Rockefellers and the members of the trilateral commission. Rather the Smiths and the members of the Huntsville (Alabama) All Star Bowling League."* Today almost half of the U.S. population is invested in the stock market. We are now the owners of the giant corporations, which have grown up around the Federal Reserve.

No it would not be prudent to ignore the history of the Federal Reserve, that's what this book is all about. We must learn from the mistakes of the past and be careful not to repeat them in the future. Therefore we are cautioned to remember the 1920s. It was a period of unprecedented economic growth. It was also a period of booming new industry and wild speculation in the stock market. We must remember the crash of 1929 and the depression throughout the 1930s. And finally, we must remember the Second World War that followed.

When we understand that what took place from 1929 to 1939 was the largest transfer of wealth that the world had ever seen, and that the events of that transfer were orchestrated by the international bankers, and when we compare what happened at that time, with the booming 1990s, we will find the same type of unprecedented economic growth and wild speculations in new industries like the volatile new tech stocks.

In fact, the 1990s is the longest period of sustained economic growth in U.S. history. When we understand this history, and what happened in the recent period of corporate scandals after 2000, we would be foolish not to consider if today's investors might be headed for the same fleecing that occurred during the 1930's. Could all this growth in the stock market, which is largely built on speculation and not sound market fundamentals, be the prelude to a crash which would make 1929 look like a walk in the park? What is the solution which will protect our wealth? What does all of this mean spiritually? We will examine these and other questions as we take a look at the advent of global stateless capital and the 1987 stock market crash.

Wall Street Culture in the 1980s

A good basic assessment of the prevailing public perception of Wall Street and the Stock Market culture during the 1980s is clearly reflected in movies like Oliver Stone's Wall Street, as well as classic books on 80s Wall Street culture like "Barbarians at the Gate," "Den of Thieves," and "Predators' Ball." They all tell the story of greed, selfishness, and corruption. The Wall Street culture of the 1980s was a major aspect of the dark side of Reagan era conservatism, this assessment is easily justifiable because the number of American Stockholders was a small minority and mostly Republican. As well, during that time, the language of Wall

Street was far more foreign to the average person than it is today.

Nevertheless, the U.S. Stock Market experienced great expansion during the 1980s. From 1980 to 1987, the Stock Market tripled in size. This was perhaps the greatest achievement of the American model of capitalism during this period. But what was the cause, and what was the price of this great expansion? What caused the great crash of 1987? As we will find out, not only were the policies of the Federal Reserve responsible for the seven year boom and 1987 bust, there were circumstances beyond even the central bankers' control which helped to bring about the wild ride of the 1980s. The cause was the dissolution of sovereign national economic borders and the advent of global stateless capital.

What is Stateless Capital?

Stateless capital is the vast stream of money which moves or travels throughout the world's international market place, and now appears to be beyond the firm control of the governments of the world or its central bankers. The origin of this stateless money can be traced back to when President Richard M. Nixon ended the gold standard by refusing to back Federal Reserve Notes with gold on August 15, 1971. When this happened, the door was left wide open for the unbridled international proliferation of inconvertible (irredeemable in precious metals) and inflationary fiat currency. Remember, politicians prefer borrowing instead of open taxation. And also don't forget; central bankers love the interest that they collect on the money that they manufacture out of nothing, which their governments borrow, making debt slaves of its citizens.

After the elimination of the gold standard, the Bretton Woods system, established in July 1944 to create a buffer among nations and allow them to regulate how capital traveled through its financial system into its domestic economy, collapsed because of growing international financial leakages. Managing international finance allotments (the amount of money loaned to a country), and controlling economic adjustments between nations (the level of economic dominance of one country's economy, compared to its neighbors), in an era of daily floating exchange rates, fortuitously became the jurisdiction of private central bankers.

With the explosion of new currency and the political and economic dissolution of border obstacles, in terms of international finance and investment throughout the remainder of the 70s, international trade, investment, and currency values were beyond the scope of governments to control. Within the decade, Forex transactions (foreign currency exchange) skyrocketed from $18 trillion a year to over $250 trillion a year. Don Snellgrove, of the *"Concord Forex Group"* (www.cfgtrading.com) tells us that: *"In 1989, Alan Greenspan made the comment that based upon previous growth of the Forex and the advent and growth of the home computer industry, the Forex is estimated to reach levels of 6.5 trillion as early as 2005. With the new Chinese Yuag appearing on the markets with such renewed strength, many market experts feel the Greenspan prediction will come true."*

But it was securities transactions (stocks, bonds, mutual funds, etc.) at that time that had a closer relationship and effect upon national economies than the Forex. During the booming 1980s, securities transactions moved ahead of banking as the direct concentrated creative motion behind the boom in global finance. International transactions in U.S. bonds and equities rocketed from 9.3% to 92.5% of U.S. economic activity, with the trend being mimicked in Japan and Germany. With equally mammoth booms in both domestic and global securities, by the mid 1980s, it was central bankers and no longer governments who became the ultimate authority in dealing with this apparently untamable beast. Peter Ducker, Professor at Claremont Graduate School, in his book, *"The Changed World Economy,"* said: *"We have no theory for an inter-national economy which is fueled by world investment rather than world trade. As a result, we do not understand the world economy and cannot predict its behavior or anticipate its trends ... We have no law for this new world economy."* Steven Solomon, in his book, *"The Confidence Game,"* had this to say: *"With economies driven increasingly by the unpredictable, sometimes violently shifting expectations of stateless capital, unelected central bankers were emerging as leaders in a crucial political confidence game with global financial markets at the fulcrum of the changed world economy ... On the evening of Black Monday, October 19, 1987, the most powerful leaders in Wall Street, Washington, and financial and political capitals throughout the world nervously awaited word of how the new Federal Reserve chairman would respond to the world's financial distress."*

Even though Greenspan commented about the dangers of the apparent speculative bubble in the market, the uncontrollable factor of stateless money moving into and out of the Stock Market, helping to create the great boom and bust of the 1980s, left chairman Greenspan apparently powerless to do anything to stop the crash of 1987. Ironically, at the same time it made the world's central bankers more illuminated and powerful than ever. At the very least, we can say that the advent of stateless capital has insured the survival of a privately controlled and unelected fourth branch of government—the Federal Reserve System. They now have total global control of the world's wealth, but the price is their cherished anonymity.

The problem central bankers are currently experiencing in dealing with the incredible amount of global capital is only a part of the reason for their pursuit of anonymity. In our telephone conversation on January 29, 2001, Princeton Professor of International Finance Peter Kenen said: *"The reason central bankers operate in mystique is to escape political pressure and avoid undermining the confidence in the systems of banking and finance."* In my research of not only the Federal Reserve but also of privately controlled central banks throughout history, I have found that these institutions have been responsible for the debauchery of currency through monopoly of fiat note issue (paper money un-backed by gold). In the results of every case, inflation and insurmountable debt has been the sullen hallmark of their tenure. That's why they seek anonymity. That's why they set out to trick the public into believing that their central bank is a part of the government by calling it the Federal Reserve when it is a privately owned institution without any reserves. If there are reserves and so many critics of the system are wrong, then why have they not allowed themselves to be audited?

I also asked Professor Kenen whether or not he believed Alan Greenspan could have contributed to the Stock Market crash in 1987 when he raised the discount rate (interest charged on loans to banks) almost immediately after taking office on August 11, 1987. His response was affirmative. I applaud Kenen for his candor, considering he works for the same university that received millions from John D. Rockefeller, one of the founders of the Federal Reserve. It should also be recalled that Princeton is also the same university where Woodrow Wilson was once President before he was chosen to become President of the United States by the international bankers and signed into law the bill which established the Federal Reserve.

The problems of the era of global capital have diminished the national sovereignty of the nations of the world and dangerously clouded the strategic balance of world power. History has shown us that there can be only one outcome when the moneychangers seize control of economics within the political process; and that is economic slavery, perpetual expansion of debt, war, and the demise of empires. Black Monday and the stock market upheavals of the recent era of corporate scandals are only a walk in the park compared to the future prospects of a New World Order wherein uncontrolled economic chaos is the order of the day.

The Bretton Woods System Transition

The Bretton Woods system of fixed currency exchange rates, with the gold-backed dollar as the government run standard, began to collapse during the 1960s and fully collapsed in 1971 when President Nixon ended the gold standard. This allowed central bankers to create as much fiat currency as they desired. This also ushered in a floating rate system which further destabilized national economies by allowing them to over-borrow, creating even greater national debt and international imbalances in order to satisfy their nefarious lust for over-consumption and deficit spending. Their solution was a central banker-controlled system of floating exchange rates under a new agreement called the International Lending Supervision Act.

The International Lending Supervision Act (ILSA 1983)

The ILSA was created as the Federal Reserves alternative to remedial Legislation, proposed by Senator William Proxmire (D-Wisconsin) that would have imposed strict bank lending limits to any single country and automatic write-off of delinquent loans, giving Congress the authority to classify IMF loans into the value-impaired categories. Paul Volcker and his central banker confederates would not allow their primary tool to correct international imbalances to become compromised, and heaven forbid that their control over debt slavery and loan restructuring would end. They successfully rode the back of the debt crisis tiger, leaving a wake of angry political currents all the way to their long desired landmark goal of implementing the kind of usury-based guidelines for less developed countries (LDC) debt negotiations, which were first used during the Latin American debt crisis. Central bankers would do well to heed the warning of John Kennedy, though he spoke of the strategic relationship between the United States and the Soviet Union, the same principle applies when he said in his inaugural address: *"Those who foolishly sought power by riding the back of the tiger ended up inside."*

The Latin American Debt Crisis

Mexico experienced an economic collapse in the summer of 1982 due to poor internal economic development and insurmountable debt. They could no longer make interest payments on their 80 billion in foreign debt. Just weeks after receiving a 3.5 billion bailout, Mexico was calling for additional loans. Brazil owed 87 billion and Argentina owed 43 billion; both defaulted and received bailouts. Remember, there are only three ways a government can raise revenue; taxation, borrowing, or printing more money. In the case of these Latin American nations, additional taxation isn't feasible because of an insufficient tax base; the people simply don't have it. Printing it will only hyper-inflate their economy and render their money even more worthless. Their only alternative is to continue borrowing to finance and perpetually restructure their debt. It's a dog chasing its tail.

The debt shock was also being felt in less developed countries in Eastern Europe, Asia, and Africa. Because of this global debt crisis, in which Latin America was rapidly and hopelessly becoming a major component, the total LDC debt ballooned to over 540 billion. Commercial banks in the U.S.,

Japan, France, and Germany held 70% of this LDC debt, while their governments held the rest. But like I've already said, the system that was set in motion by the likes of J. P. Morgan, Paul Warburg, Nelson Aldrich, and other plutocrats, has taken on a life of its own. Today, as well as during the Latin American debt crisis, central bankers are virtually powerless to effectively control the dynamics of this New World Order's international economy of their own creation. Therefore the banks themselves were vulnerable to the greatest risk associated with the fractional reserve policy—panicked runs because of overexposure. The greatest risk to governments was loss of economic sovereignty and the perpetuation of debt slavery. The harsh cold reality, which central bankers can't afford for the public to ever fully realize, is that we are caught in the grips of a self cannibalizing system that they can no longer control.

One creative, albeit extremely oppressive alternative policy to the current debt-restructuring programs that central bankers are now offering is debt for equity swaps to those nations that can no longer make interest payments on their loans. In other words, when they can no longer make interest payments on loans that were created out of nothing at all, these debtor nations must now sign over all rights to their natural resources to a greed-inspired group of privately owned central banks. The nations of the world have borrowed from the beast to fulfill the lust of their flesh. Now the devil is ready to foreclose.

When Banks Lend Too Much

Lending to developing nations escalated far beyond any prudent economic assessment, mainly because governments allocated LDC debt financing to the jurisdiction of private central bankers whose true motivation was and always is profit. According to Merril Stevenson in his article entitled, *"A Game of Skill As Well: Survey of International Banking," The Economist*, March 21, 1987: *"Between 1970 and 1987 the profits on international operations (mostly LDC loans) of America's largest seven banks soared from 22% to 60% of total earnings. When questioned about such crazy lending, Citibank chairman Walter Wriston sarcastically responded, 'Countries don't go broke; unlike a company, countries don't declare bankruptcy and disappear. My loans are as good as a T-Bill.'"*

So how did the Third World debt crisis contribute to the global capital problem? The answer is, too much of the foreign borrowing was wasted in various forms of corruption. The corruption came in the form of poor investments, theft by corrupt government officials, and reckless attempts to shelter their loans from runaway domestic inflation by reinvesting their loans back into the U.S. markets. These were the prime contributors to the problem of untamed stateless capital and the creation of what economists came to call the superdollar of the late 1980s. Merril Stevenson in *"The Economist"* estimated from 1975 up to half of the 10 major LDCs debt in Latin America (some 300 billion) left their countries in favor of more positive yields in capital and financial markets abroad. That money is called flight capital. It would return to circulate as new stateless or hot money. This is money that public and private investors take out of a country in a heartbeat if their investment in that country is not panning out. No central banker can control that phenomenon; they can only react to it, usually with some inadequate ad hoc response.

I for one believe that the LDC debt crisis and the increase in the global capital juggernaut was created by, or at the very least, is used by central bankers for the purpose of overwhelming governments and thereby taking control of the international lending process. This was all accomplished in secrecy by central bankers and their nefarious poodles in government. They created a problem then offered the solution, which would bring about their desired result. The post-Bretton Woods system of involuntary lending (lending without Congressional approval) under diabolical accords like the ILSA allow the optimization of economic slavery and debauchery of currency through the use of dishonest weights and measures on a global scale. (Lev. 19:35)

Bringing Down the Superdollar

As we have already said, most LDC's loans were reinvested into U.S. markets. This caused the dollar to become extremely over-valued. In other words, the dollar became the superdollar. The superdollar created unprecedented international economic imbalances as America depended on the money from foreigners to finance its debt. In addition, because U.S. taxpayers unwittingly guarantee LDC's loans, we become co-debtors in their growing debt crisis. The U.S. deficit became so great that the U.S. economic status shifted from the greatest creditor nation to the largest debtor nation on the face of the earth.

The problem now was how to bring the dollar to a soft landing. Although the dollar-centered Bretton Woods system no longer existed, the dollar was still the most potent signal for changes in international investment allocation and calibration. The dollar's status was and still is the greatest influence on international growth, inflation, and employment. In the final analysis, global flight capital into the U.S. created a false notion of prosperity in America and recession in the rest of the world. Therefore balances had to be made. But who would establish the proper regulations which would bring the superdollar to a soft landing? Certainly it could not be President Reagan. Like most U.S. presidents, Reagan had little or no knowledge or interest in the dollar's status abroad. According to Steven Solomon in *"The Confidence Game,"* ex-Deputy Treasury Secretary Tim McNamar who prepared Reagan for international economics meetings said: *"Reagan lacked certain bodies of economic knowledge ... in terms of the dollar's status; he only knew people called him to bitch about it. The Reagan/Bush administration believed the superdollar status was a vote of confidence from the free market and the cure for Europe's financial maladies was the Anglo-Saxon style financial deregulation and other U.S. supply side strategies."* I wonder if our leaders are being described in the book of Isaiah 56:10-11: *"His watchmen are blind, they are all without knowledge; they are all dumb dogs, they cannot bark; dreaming, lying down, loving to slumber. The dogs have a mighty appetite; they never have enough. The shepherds also have no understanding; they have all turned to their own way, each to his own gain, one and all."*

We should now see how dangerous the combined forces of government ignorance, indifference, and corruption, along with the 80s explosion of global capital, were in creating unprecedented global imbalances and the ad hoc regulatory measures of central bankers in the post-Bretton Woods era of floating exchange rates and involuntary lending. These forces eventually caused the dollar to crash and burn instead of landing safely and softly, and brought the world to the brink of financial collapse while triggering the 1987 stock market crash.

The Final Countdown to Black Monday

In testimony before the U.S. Senate Committee on Banking, Housing, and Urban Affairs in February of 1988, on the 1987 stock market crash, Alan Greenspan's statement clearly indicated his prior awareness of the state of the world's chaotic economy, and the impending collapse of the world's markets. He was fully aware of the extraordinary forces, both at home and abroad, which caused the U.S. stock market to soar throughout the decade. He said: *"Something had to snap. If it didn't happen in October, it would have happened soon thereafter. The market plunge was an accident waiting to happen."*

When Japanese investors in America began shifting from bonds into equities after the April bond market crash, this caused the delicate bond market to become radically destabilized. The market began a period of accelerated and dramatic expansion due to a rapid rise of Leveraged Buyouts (LBOs) and corporate takeovers, which we will discuss later. What made this rise so dangerous was that LBOs at that time were financed to a large extent by stateless capital, mainly from returning LDC loan reinvestments. These factors, along with a three year long frozen discount rate, were the remaining driving forces behind the runaway expansion of the market.

Greenspan's public objective as the newly named Fed chairman was to bring stabilization to the market and establish his credibility with Wall Street. In my opinion, the main point to consider with his solution to this problem, which was raising the discount rate in order to slow the economy down and avoid the possible catastrophic fall from a stratospheric peak is that, historically, this credit contractual maneuver has been used to trigger crashes, recessions, and sometimes depressions. Throughout history, the ultimate beneficiaries in this type of policy, which allows private central banks to manufacture, loan, and charge interest on money which they create out of nothing, has never been the people, it is always the bank.

Another force, moving America perilously closer to the impending crash, was the October news of the House Ways and Means Committee's intention of eliminating key corporate tax benefits. These were the same elements within the tax code which had helped to encourage LBOs in the early and mid 1980s. Congress was hoping to safely guide the corporate markets and restore some balance in global investing. The move was too little-too late. Not only that, where their money is concerned, investors lack a healthy sense of true patriotism, so they ran for cover just as they historically have done whenever the government tries to impose reasonable restraint on corporations. Remember, in the Wall Street culture of the 1980s, people weren't concerned with what was good for the country; their only concern was their pockets. Bottom line, this move significantly helped to precipitate the crash.

The U. S. Commerce Department then announced a whopping quarterly trade deficit of over 15 billion dollars. This triggered Japanese investors to sell their U.S. bonds and the rest of the world to mimic their panic. Pandemonium began to take hold on markets around the world. In three days' time, from October 14 to 16, the Dow Jones index fell over 250 points with record volume trading. The countdown was down to mere seconds.

As the final seconds ticked away, domestic banks were losing money to the competition from foreign banks chasing global capital. Corporate bankruptcies and defaults were setting postwar records. The government's ad hoc policy in response to Reagan's suppressed S&L scandal called for deregulating the industry and backing even more unscrupulous loans. Fed ex-chairman Paul Volcker called the government's response *"kamikaze banking."* Nevertheless the Federal Reserve started collecting interest on a $40 billion dollar S&L bailout made with money they created out of nothing. The S&L Association of California said that the rise in interest rates during the prior week caused it to fail. Ultimately, the central bank is always the winner.

All these things were too much for the market to bear. On Monday, October 19, 1987, the Stock Market crashed, losing almost two years of its gains. At the closing bell the market was down 508 points. Like President Herbert Hoover at the 1929 Stock Market crash, the most important thing President Reagan had to do at that point was to calm and reassure the world that everything was all right. If Reagan ever was a great actor, now was the time he really had to prove it. The public had to believe that the economy was still sound, and that our capital and financial markets were still safe. But they weren't. Just like 1929, a massive transfer of wealth had occurred. Wall Street was in a panic. If the public lost all confidence in the system the damage would be prolonged and even more severe than it already was.

The NYSE Dow Jones Index fall to 22.6 on Black Monday was more forceful than the crash of 1929. It was the result of a deeper ignominy within the post-war global economy. One big part of the problem was and still is stateless money. The postwar era of central banker dominance over a segregated national banking system was being transmuted into a desegregated national banking system, of which they apparently have no control. In other words, after 1945 banking was separated by the borders of nations, but by 1987 it had truly gone global; therefore, mistakes made by bankers, and the vulnerability of banks, were now shown to have an immediate and catastrophic world wide ripple effect. No nation would ever again be immune to the economic misfortune of its neighbors because of the advent of stateless money, and central bankers were at a loss on what to do about it.

One of the most celebrated post 1987 crash studies, Nicholas Brady's *"Presidential Task Force on Market Mechanisms,"* summarized technical failures to keep pace with the stateless money revolution: *"Institutional and regulatory structures designed for separate marketplaces were incapable of dealing with a precipitate inter-market decline which brought the financial system to the brink.*" Another part of the problem was outlined in the September 8, 1990 issue of *"The Economist,"* when Norman Macrae said: *"The tacit offer from governments for about 30 years after 1945 was that they would allow banks a stable high level of profit by ensuring that depositors had few other places than banks in which to put their liquid funds, and that borrowers would have few other places from which they could respectively borrow ... In return for governments' blessing on these cartels, bankers agreed to become governments' poodles in nefarious ways.*" In other words, from 1945 restrained market growth was government policy under the old Bretton Woods system. As the system slowly collapsed so did market restraints. The world witnessed the ramifications of corporations and investors taking a mile of the world market, when in the past they were only given an inch.

The bible says that a leopard cannot change his spots. Throughout history the monetary scientists have always used economic chaos as a means of transferring the wealth of the people into their private coffers. With the absence of scholarly criticism emanating from universities, which have mostly been bought off with heavy endowments from the Money Trust, both before and after the creation of the Federal Reserve System, credible inquiry into the possibility of the kinds of historical injustices imposed on the working class has slowly become compromised. Can a leopard change his spots? Have the moneychangers really lost control? Or are they continuing to manipulate boom and bust cycles for their own gain? Is the world being victimized by economic exploitation? It must be remembered that any major crisis, whether naturally occurring or contrived, has been often used by governments as a pretext for expansion of its authority over the people. Check out history and judge for yourself.

Metaphysical Reflections

The segregated nationalistic control which central bankers had over the largely isolated markets before the crash of '87, contrasted by the internationally liberated global market era after the Black Monday period, is one of the events which marks the change between the old world order (OWO), and the new world order (NWO). Yes, the New World Order is already here. Its manifestation is plain to see for those who understand what is going on. It typifies the old and new religious covenants in the bible. The open yet private role of central bankers in America since the establishment of the Federal Reserve System, typifies how the priests ruled Israel, ecclesiastically, politically, and economically, with both an open ceremonial and a hidden plutocratic agenda during the time of the old covenant with its' mosaic law. The hidden plutocracy of private central bankers was and still is their reason for seeking anonymity, just as the oppressive economic influences of the priests in post-diluvian Israel were kept cloaked by their dignified role in society. Indeed, the carnal mind has always operated in this self-same vain modus operandi of self-protection.

The Law of Moses contained strict rules, which isolated Israel among the nations. The ancient Hebrew law was a two edged sword—life for obedience, death for disobedience. (Deut. 28th Chapter) In like manner, the laws that governed the U.S. financial markets isolated them from the powerful influence of global capital's two-edged sword. Ironically, living under the Mosaic Law isolates the consciousness from the powerful inward influence of spirit, which also is a two-edged sword—life for obedience and death for disobedience to the still small voice within. Foreign capital at work in America can build the market tremendously, if there is compliance with a new and more perfect law, requiring equitability, and fairness in all areas of international economic intercourse. Conversely, foreign capital can abandon and wreck our economy when inequity and unfairness exists between the world's markets. In like manner, following the inner voice, which I-believe is Spirit under the new covenant, can build the consciousness and establish great spiritual wealth. Not following this inward mandate of the new covenant can result in chaos & spiritual abandonment. We must never forget that the events of our time and every epoch in history reflect the state of the moral and spiritual consciousness of mankind. (Rom. 1:19-20)

Before we move on to examine the great bull market of the 1990s we must discuss one other area of economics, which greatly contributed to the destabilization and fragility of the pre-crash 1980s markets, the leveraged buyout or corporate take-over.

LBOs

One of the most widely covered financial developments of the 1980s is the leveraged buyout (LBO). Intended to cut the public shareholders out of huge profits, investors would take a company private by buying out the public shares, then selling it off after retooling or dismantling the company.

The most prominent practitioners of this sullen art were Republican plutocrats like Henry Kravits and his colleagues at Kohlberg, Kravits & Roberts. KKR were agents initially operating on behalf of private investors with so much success that they soon tapped institutional investors, including public employee pension funds. With this acquisition capital KKR funds grew from 980 million in 1984, to 5.6 billion in 1987.

Michael Milken was another important figure in the 1980s era of leveraged buyouts and junk bond kings. Milken was convicted and served 36-40 months in a California penitentiary for SEC violations even after both he and Drexel Burnham were browbeaten into a 1.3 billion dollar settlement by the SEC and U.S. attorney. His modern day robber baron tactics are the subject of the book, *"Den of Thieves,"* by James Stewart—a classic on the corruption of Wall Street in the 80s.

But even in the 80s climate of unbridled avarice, there were some people who were still gullible enough to believe Milken and his associates got a bum rap. In an article for *"Contra Mundum"* entitled, *"It's Not Nice to Make Money,"* by Mark Ahlseen, the author argues: *"The 1980s has been labeled the decade of greed. Advocates of this view contend that abuses of all kinds abounded unimpeded by the Reagan administration. Only the vigilance of sincere politicians and media elite saved the American people from catastrophe. The primary abuse occurred on Wall Street in the frenzy of corporate takeovers. And Michael Milken epitomized this greed in his willingness to finance the corporate raiders. Unfortunately, Americans have come to accept this charge and to blame corporate greed for all the financial problems of the 1980s. Daniel Fischel's book 'Payback: The Conspiracy to Destroy Michael Milken and His Financial Revolution' seeks to give another explanation. The author is a professor at the University of Chicago Law School with extensive knowledge of financial markets. The title of the book is somewhat misleading in that it focuses on more than just the Milken case. The author's basic premise is that the 1980s witnessed an increase in the effort to fuel class envy on the part of liberals and a backlash of old, established money trying to protect itself from upstarts like Milken. Throw in a government willing to change the rules in the middle of the game and you have the unsavory prosecutions that took place at the end of the 1980s."*

But not everyone was fooled. Dr. David Bronner, the CEO of the Retirement Systems of Alabama's successful public pension fund, which has made billions in LBOs, called Milken and the boys *"rich pool hall sharks."* These guys were not merely the object of nervous Wall Street witch hunters, these guys inflicted serious harm on this nation. They were nothing short of economic terrorists. To me, the whole idea of leveraged buyouts is motivated by greed. But such were the heroes of the 1980s Wall Street culture. In a curious way it is reminiscent of the twisted public adoration of Mafia dons.

Another 1980s billionaire, who considered himself a latter-day Rockefeller, was Ron Perelman. His ruthless leveraged buyouts acquired more than 8 billion in assets during this period for his holding company, Mac Andrews & Forbes. Their portfolio includes Revlon, Marvel Entertainment, Fleer Trading Cards, the Coleman Company, New World Communications, First Nationwide Bank, National Health, and Consolidated Cigar Corporation. Needless to say, in the 1980s' LBO world, the public shareholder was usually the loser, while megalomaniac conservative plutocrat corporate raiders like Perelman amassed great fortunes by aspiring to emulate the sinister workings of the Rockefellers and the rest of the architects of 20th century economic slavery. Others include the Texas billionaire oil baron turned corporate raider T. Boone Pickens. Pickens was the first raider to get the backing of Michael Milken. He was also the first to make the cover of Fortune Magazine, making runs at the likes of Gulf Oil and Phillips Petroleum. He was the most hated man in corporate America. Carl Icahn, another 80s billionaire raider, who used leveraged buyouts to take companies private, then sold them off at substantial profits, is still making headlines today, most recently with the sale of Nabisco holdings to R.J. Reynolds Tobacco Holdings for 9.8 billion.

All of these icons of the 1980s money culture were political conservatives. They represented the public's idea of

Wall Street's exclusionist nature in the 80s. Unlike Wall Street's democratized 90s icons, they made money for themselves while often times abusing the now new Wall Street tycoon, the little guy. Nevertheless, it would be a great mistake for citizens in this democracy to allow today's democratized Wall Street culture, political differences, personal agenda, or any other societal or media driven scenery to distract them from their weightiest economic problem. The problem is international bankers operating through the Federal Reserve System and the rest of the world's central banks are transferring untold economic wealth from the poor to the super rich. They now have such immense power over the markets that with a single statement, markets all over the world react without controllable limits to their effect on the prosperity of millions of people all over the world. Remember, fearing the power of central banks, Thomas Jefferson said: *"I sincerely believe that banking institutions are more dangerous to our liberties than standing armies. The issuing power should be taken from the banks and restored to the people to whom it properly belongs."*

We are now engulfed in another recession after one of the longest periods of market growth and economic prosperity in U.S. history. We should ask the Congress to assuage our anxiety and bring an end to these unstable and disruptive cycles of boom and bust by abolishing the Federal Reserve System, and return to following the monetary and economic structural mandates of the Constitution, as well as the wise admonishments of Jefferson, Madison, Jackson, Lincoln, Franklin and other fighters of privately owned central banks and their economic tyranny.

The Alleged U.S. / Japanese Central Bank Involvement in the Election of George Bush 1988

The political complexion of America has been manipulated by the central banking process throughout our history of failed experiments with privately owned central banks. The process is as certain as the operation of DNA within cells. The outcome of elections, not only in the U.S. but all over the world, has been very greatly influenced by secret back door central bank policy. Jimmy Carter blamed ex-Fed chairman Paul Volcker's handling of the economy for undermining his re-election bid in 1980. George Bush lamented over the tight money policy of the Greenspan Fed. Bill Clinton leaned totally on Greenspan to steer the economy and took the credit for the 1990s bull market.

A few months after the crash, on January 13, 1988, the new Japanese Prime Minister Takeshita told President Reagan that unless the dollar rallied Japanese dollar investment losses could exceed the 15% threshold for public disclosure. That would trigger a massive international retreat from the dollar bringing the crisis to a perilous new level. This set the tone for serious bilateral diplomacy between the Reagan White House and the Bank of Japan (BOJ) in an attempt to avoid the dollar crisis long enough to get Bush elected in 1988.

On January 19, 1988 Secretary James Baker could only watch Alan Greenspan use maximum freedom in negotiating the economy away from the much feared recession and stabilize proper dollar value with the G7 (group of seven leading industrial nations). There were many in the financial markets who knew that the initiatives of the June 21, 1988 G7 summit in Toronto were the product of clandestine back door agreements made by James Baker, Alan Greenspan and Japanese Finance Minister Kiichi Miyazawa for the express purpose of electing Bush to the U.S. Presidency in 1988. Solomon Brothers' analyst Nick Sargen said: *"The dollars' support was the result of a conspiracy."* In his book, ***"The Confidence Game,"*** Steve Solomon said: *"There was no doubt that Japanese and foreign officials preferred Republican Bush over Democrat Michael Dukakis. The BOJ in fact did target the dollar, against its better judgment. The BOJ campaign to anchor dollar interest and exchange rates reached extraordinary lengths in the summer. Inflationary expectations were causing money to leak away from Japan's domestic money markets, where interest rates were held artificially low through unofficial BOJ "whispers" to tanshi, or money brokers."*

The Baker/Greenspan proposal was for the Bank of Japan (BOJ) to keep Japanese discount rates low enough to allow the river of Japanese capital into U.S. markets to continue. Any disruption before the 1988 presidential election would undermine the dollar, and thereby it would undermine public confidence in the economy. We are all familiar with the phrase, "It's the Economy Stupid." James Baker, George Bush, and his Japanese supporters were very aware that Americans vote with their pocketbooks during peace time. In other words, when the economy goes, so does the incumbent party. In 1988 Kemper Financial Services Chief Economist David Hale understood the secrecy and weight of Japanese investments into the U.S. securities market and the effect of their demands on the U.S. economy and political process. He believed Japanese life insurance portfolio managers should go ahead and address Americans on the political effect of Japanese money on key U.S. economic policy, because for damn sure, the candidates weren't going to do it. In the April 18, 1988 issue of the ***"Wall Street Journal,"*** he said: *"Such a program would probably give American voters more information about the direction of economic policy after 1988 than they appear likely to get from the candidates themselves."*

One major point of significance of the Japanese/ American dollar conspiracy is the fact that Japan became the unofficial 51st state, whose unofficial delegates were 100% Republican. The result of this unofficial Japanese/American accord would be the fact that U.S. citizens would be allowed to continue living beyond their means on borrowed Japanese money at the expense of unborn American taxpayers. Steven Solomon tells us that the ex-Ministry of Finance Director of Japan Takashi Hosoni said: *"The United States hates to adopt any kind of stringent monetary policy. The so-called floating rate system is best for the United States to issue whatever amount of currency it wants without any responsibility to pay back."*

According to Professor William Branson in Pat Choate's recent book, ***"Agents of Influence,"*** documenting the growing influence of Japanese money in American politics, there are two possible outcomes for U.S. debt to Japan: *"One view is that the Japanese are in deep trouble since all their investments are in the United States and the U.S. will inflate it away. The other view says that the Japanese are gaining a dominant position in the U.S. economy and will eventually control the politicians—buy a congressman,"* or as it turned out, a U.S. President.

Almost as soon as Bush was elected the honeymoon was over. The powerful yet fragile economic and political relationship between the U.S. and Japan began to degenerate. The dollar began to fall. The tension between America and Japan became likened to the strategic relationship between the U.S. and the U.S.S.R. during the cold war. The survival of both sides depended on sober reasoning. The jockeying for economic and political advantages in the face of prolonged external economic imbalances had degenerated into a dangerous game of brinkmanship. Both sides threatened to deploy monetary weapons that could bring about mutually assured economic destruction. For example, many books and articles have outlined the Washington Consensus during the 1980s, but in an article in the *"Institutional Investor Journal"* by Cary Reich, entitled *"The Privatization of Paul Volcker,"* Federal Reserve chairman Paul Volcker's notoriety for a strong liberalization and privatization policy, driven often times by brinksmanship, is candidly highlighted. In this case, Volcker constantly warned Japan: *"We see a big deficit with Japan, and we say, Goddamn it, you Japanese better open up your markets."* A trade reciprocity bill in the U.S. Senate ultimately followed this tense period in the winter of '90-'91 to open Japan's markets. The chilling reply of Japanese Ministry of Finance and Vice Minister for International Affairs, Makoto Utsumi, was a dangerous threat to deploy its economic weapon of mass destruction, cutting off capital flows into U.S. addicted markets.

Why is this stuff important? Because the public should be allowed to understand the threats it faces. The simple truth of the matter is that people should know that economic weapons are just as devastating as nuclear weapons. To contain these threats, sometimes rules, due process, and even democracy are compromised. Back door deals that circumvent the established diplomatic protocols are implemented. Sometimes the consequences of these kinds of trade war actions can have globally catastrophic ramifications.

You would think that the effect of global capital would discipline and strengthen the virtue of governments, and turn out to be a boon in capitalist societies. But central bankers have used its propensity to extreme volatility, political maneuvering, and chaos to take total control of world economic affairs in a highly politicized environment. The global capital revolution has made the world's central bankers the undisputed architects and over-lords of the New World Order. The constant striving for a plutocratic New World Order by men and the institutions they represent also shows the essential nature of man—always striving for self-sufficiency, relying not on the better angels of his nature, but the often times vain carnal riches of his own intellect. (Proverbs 3:5)

A New International Policy for Stateless Money

With growing world-wide economic imbalances, sky-rocketing third world debt, and increasing domestic corporate, bank, and S&L fragility, all converging by the summer of '86, the prospect of a world-wide economic meltdown was imminent. But all of these problems had a common denominator that was almost unsolvable. The international common denominator to the multitude of problems central bankers faced in the summer of 1986, was trying to pilot markets and institutions that had become world-wide in scope, but were still being regulated on a closed, isolated, country by country basis. A new international standard policy for the new hot money era had to be implemented.

National and even regional borders had been reduced to mere lines on a map, and from a practical perspective, national economic divisions that those lines would seem to indicate, meant nothing. The sloppy regulations that were quickly implemented from crisis to crisis left a very uneven playing field among financial institutions, as well as capital and financial markets of different nationalities. Steve Solomon in the book, *"The Confidence Game,"* said: *"Japan was the most prominent regulatory lump in the 1980s global financial landscape. Where a U.S. bank had to raise $6 of capital for every $100 loan it made, its Japanese competitor was required to hold only $2 or $3. Armed with this huge cost advantage, Japanese banks' share of international banking business*

catapulted from 17% to 38% from 1983 to 1988. U.S. banks'
share fell from over 26% to under 15%."

The playing field among the world's privately owned central banks had to be made equal. As long as one country's central bank was disadvantaged by unequal standards, problems associated with competition for fair and equal access to international business would persist. Likewise, the corrective reaction taken by those banks in the disadvantaged underdog position would illicit retaliatory corrective actions by the competing banks. This banking cold war could only end when globally accepted standards for bank reserve requirements and universal money definitions were achieved. (Note: Today's reserve requirement in the Federal Reserve and the Bank of Canada is 0%. This means the requirements of reserve deposit to loan ratio being 0% now allows these central banks to create unlimited amounts of money out of nothing and loan it out with interest. This is the ultimate system of usury, based on the principle of dishonest weights and measures. (Lev. 19:35)

A New Global Monetary Standard Emerges

The meetings that brought about the world's first protocols on the various aspects of a new world-wide monetary standard were held secretly between officials from the Federal Reserve and the Bank of England from October to December 1986. The central bankers quickly reacted and came up with their accords after the American Congress began to perceive that the U.S. economy was being held hostage by Japan's projectionist policies. Government intervention was unacceptable because a Congressional trade war would threaten central banker anonymity and undermine public confidence in the system. The result was an Anglo-American center of gravity accord between the Japanese and German officials. The

German rigorous and strict regulatory credit measures, contrasted by Japan's extreme loose credit position, would have to find compromise in the Anglo-American flexible approach.

Unilateral accords were reached in Brussels among G10 (group of ten major industrialized nations) on June 23 and 24, 1987. The solution was a twin-leveled formula mandating capital assessments (the value of one country's currency as it compares to others) for each bank to be based equally on both pure capital (realized assets such as real estate and precious metals, which is the best quality), which was to German and Swiss liking, as well as assets based on unrealized capital gains (soft money like securities) which assuaged the position of the Bank of Japan (BOJ).

Final endorsement of global capital standards were ratified In July 1988 among G10 Governors. The agreements were reached and adopted without official vote or documentation. The fragile agreement rested solely upon the so-called central banker code of honor. These agreements made it possible for central bankers to create as much money as they wanted out of absolutely nothing at all, and charge interest on its use, as long as they submitted to peer review. Steven Solomon tells us that Bank of Canada Governor John Crow said: *"There is no limit to the imagination of people to invent hybrid instruments that might count as capital. Now they must submit to peer review."* Keep in mind, these so-called international economic protectionist accords created just enough economic order at the end of the Reagan administration to prevent undermining the chances for Bush to be elected President of the United States in November 1988. This would be followed by a resulting over-lending boom in the real estate markets of the U.S., Japan, and the U.K., which led to the dangerous price deflation of these real financial assets; as well, the lending boom contributed significantly to the growing third world debt crisis. These events made the 1990s a period of low-intensity depression, or what economists have termed a contained depression, and would ultimately cost Bush the election in 1992.

Again, I must say that I am persuaded that the apparent problem of global stateless capital was created by the world's privately owned central banks. Whether the problem arose by accident or by design, it has been useful in advancing their plutocratic agenda, which has always been the relentless pursuit of world domination through the sullen art of usury. It must never be forgotten that the practitioners of this craft have never allowed the principles of patriotism, nationalism, or humanism to preclude their reckless avarice. As long as we the people choose to allow private central banks to have a monopoly on the issue of our money there will always be debt, inflation, and global economic imbalances. We must never forget that, historically, these economic maladies have been used to extend the power of private central bankers toward their current total control over the economic and political dynamics of the world. Their fait money, along with dissolution of national economic borders, has helped shape the world's sovereign economic landscape into a privately controlled global economic environment, which genders the catastrophic shifts in focus and mania of the global investor era. The arrhythmia of the global economic heartbeat has endowed central bankers with total control of the wealth of nations in the New World Order.

The apostle John saw the unleashing of this leviathan in a divine vision while on the Isle of Patmos in the Aegean Sea in AD 96 as recorded in the bibles' book of Revelations. John described it as Mystery Babylon, an ecclesiastical, political, and economic system. John saw its ultimate demise in Rev. 18:11-24. He also sees and describes the state of our current economic slavery in Rev. 13:16-18: *"And he causeth all, both small and great, rich and poor, free and bond, to receive a mark in their right hand, or in their foreheads: and that no man might buy or sell, save he that had the mark, or the name of the beast, or the number of his name. Here is wisdom. Let him that hath understanding count the number of the beast: for it is the number of a man; and his number is six hundred threescore and six."* (Note: the number six in Hebrew theology represents the flesh.) These same symbols which John describes, also typify the carnal mindset which creates such greed, as well as the negative attributes described in Gal. 5th chapter. Whether one believes in a divine creator or not, it doesn't take a hell of a stretch for a person armed with a basic understanding of the secret history and recent activity of the world's privately owned central banks, to see the allegorical symbolism and agree with these correlations. Avarice has built the New World Order and avarice shall be its destruction. Although Congress does have the authority to abolish the Federal Reserve, and restore the economic sovereignty of the United States, it will likely never happen. Divine intervention seems to be the only thing that can bring an end to this economic slavery and global usury.

The Hegemony of the U.S. Dollar: the Silent Influence on the Iraq War

Thomas Jefferson once said: *"If a nation expects to be ignorant and free, it expects what never was and never will be. The people cannot be safe without information. When the press is free, and every man can read, all is safe."* The posture of the mainstream media, insisting that the war in Iraq is not about oil, is only partly true. War is a very complex phenomenon, brought about by many extenuating circumstances. Oil is a major, albeit not exclusive factor in the war in Iraq. What the American people are not being told is that one of the prime reasons for the war in Iraq is the Euro. It's no secret that money has always played a major role in the advent and justification for war. Here, as in most cases in recorded history, money has once again laid claim for all those with eyes to see, as the chief reason the hawks are seeking their prey. These denials about the reasons for this war are as unconvincing as Colin Powell's claim that Iraqi oil will be held in trusteeship for the Iraqi people. That's exactly what the League of Nations promised Levant when it allowed France and Great Britain to establish a presence in Palestine, Trans-Jordan, Syria, and Lebanon after World War I. History has shown that the trusteeship didn't materialize.

So the question is, how could a simple monetary unit like the Euro pose so great a threat to the U.S.? The answer is really simple. OPEC wants the Euro in exchange for purchase of its oil. They no longer want to see oil continue as a dollar-backed commodity. As we have learned, in the post-World War II, post-Bretton Woods economic era, and specifically since the end of the gold standard in 1971, the U.S. dollar emerged as the standard global monetary instrument. All payments of international debt, and international transactions, including oil purchases, were done with dollars. Therefore the United States alone has enjoyed the luxury of servicing its debt with its dollars, which are created out of nothing at all by the Federal Reserve. As long as the dollar was the world's strongest currency, every other nation was forced to exchange their currency for U.S. dollars so that they can finance trade and make payments on their debts to the world's privately owned central banks. As well, every other country in the world has been forced into maintaining dollars as reserves in their central banks to back their softer currencies. This is called

"Dollar Hegemony." This dominance of the dollar has been the greatest depressive factor on all other nations of the earth because a significant portion of their purchasing power and currency value is lost when developing nations have to exchange their soft (weaker) currencies for hard (stronger) currencies (dollars) in order to service hopelessly insurmountable and perpetually expanding debts.

The big problem lies in the fact that the dollar has been in chronic decline in value against the Euro over the last 24 months, and now stands in jeopardy of losing its precious hegemony. If, therefore, war is required to enforce prudence in regard to the pace and sequence of an inevitable paradigm shift in global monetary standards toward the Euro, all else is only of marginal consequence to the Federal Reserve. Because if the United States is forced by Saddam Hussein and his oil rich Middle Eastern confederates, into exchanging its dollars for Euros in order to buy oil from OPEC, the U.S. economy would be terminally damaged. This is just one reason that prices at the gas pump have increased so drastically. It is not the only reason for the recent spike in gas prices; Wall Street speculation on oil prices, increased demand for gas, especially in China and the developing Pacific Rim, cuts in OPEC production, and restrictions on tapping American oil reserves, have all contributed to the astronomical rise in gas prices.

The threat to dollar hegemony, exacerbated by Washington's sluggish fiscal stimulus policy, is rendering our swollen national debt unserviceable. Current fiscal stimulus policies should be enacted with extreme caution. Finally, the Federal Reserve Chairman Alan Greenspan, in an address before the Senate Banking Committee, is now saying, any future tax cuts should be *"budget neutral,"* or essentially offset by spending cuts to avoid future negative stimulus to growth and further weakening of the dollar. Moreover, because products are brought to market by trucks, which require gas and oil, the sudden increased expense would create a devastating inflationary ripple in the U.S. economy. In short, America would experience an economic meltdown likened to the crisis already well underway in many third world countries.

Chapter Ten

The New Economy and the Creation of the 1990s Bull Market

The Post Crash Economy

*W*hat immediately followed the crash was the same thing that follows every collapse of the economy—debt. Early in 1992 Alan Greenspan said: *"During the last five years we've experienced an extraordinary debt build up followed by a decline in the value of the assets (real estate) used to collateralize it. To repair balance sheets means that instead of consumption and investment, people are paying off their debts. Since it'll take a long time to get back to equilibrium, the economy can't move forward."*

The Fed's response to the post crash stagnation was to artificially lower interest rates to entice investors back into the market. The individual speculator responded to the point of becoming reckless, taking on tremendous debt and exposure.

Along with this, the myopic zeal of fund managers, brokerage houses, banks, and other institutional investor services, toward the democratization of Wall Street, without regard for undue speculative risks for the neophyte investor class, also greatly contributed to the economic bubble and its ultimate burst by the end of the 1990s. The outcome of the sudden democratization and liberalization of Wall Street, for the average American with his hard earned savings in his hand, was like a lamb stumbling onto a pack of lions—a blood bath. In the computer and information age, this is what can occur when interest rates are low—like they were when Volcker cut the discount rate and sustained it throughout the early 1980s under a climate of growing and unsustainable global economic imbalances. Artificially low interest rates, for the purpose of enticing investors, can result in fueling catastrophic market adjustments, in an ad hoc attempt to keep the stock market from a catastrophic fall from a stratospheric peak. Rather than a soft landing, the outcome may often result in crashes, panics, and recessions, in turn, generating tremendous debt. (*Keep in mind, a privately owned central bank makes money by collecting interest on these debts. Also keep in mind the fact that they are the ones who provide the incentive to recklessly, or otherwise, consume and invest.*) It was these factors, along with a post-war downsizing of the military and rising oil prices because of the Persian Gulf crisis, which contributed to stagnating the economic bust cycle that cost Bush the 1992 election.

On December 19, 1991, Alan Greenspan's corrective measures, part of which was lowering the discount rate one full percentage point to 3.5%, the lowest since the Kennedy years, would open the door to another cycle of economic boom. This time it would be the longest sustained period of economic growth in U.S. history, which was known as "The Clinton years." Accordingly, President Clinton left office with a 65% job approval rating, one of the highest in U.S. history.

By the end of Clinton's second term of office, the market began correcting itself. The over-valued stocks on the NASDAQ began coming down and investors became nervous. The dollar had become so debased until it didn't take much lack of confidence to send investors, both foreign and domestic, running for cover. Today, as Greenspan said then, the public is so mired in debt from losses incurred during the great bullish 90s, that it cannot support the American corporate base. Corporations have opted to flee the carnage and move overseas, leaving the American labor market high and dry. The point of this chapter is this—if America only understood how these cycles of boom and bust have been haphazardly instigated by the Federal Reserve System in this country, and the instability and volatility that global capital brings to the market, then like me, the country as a whole would have known and understood that another devastating bust cycle was a mathematical certainty.

The Decade of the Little Guy: The New Stock Market Tycoon

Daniel Gross, in the book, *"Bull Run,"* tells us of the changes in the socio-economic complexion of Wall Street's players. He recounts the wake of the stock market crash of 1987, pointing out how: *"the entire financial system, from underwriters to Mutual Fund companies, from commercial banks to the financial news media, retooled and restructured to serve people like Appel (a cab driver) and 84 million other Americans who own stocks, to ply them with information and services, and to make them feel as if they are insiders in one of the greatest and longest running confidence games around; the 1990s bull market."*

Worthy of being called the greatest market expansion in U.S. history, the 1990s was a decade of unparalleled liberalization. Brand new companies like E-Trade, starting in

1992 with no business, are now worth more than 1.5 billion in assets. Gross tells us that in 1992 Paine Webber CEO Richard Marron characterized the 90s as *"the decade of the little guy."* By the end of the decade, almost 50% of America had become stockholders; up from 20% in 1990; that's more stockholders than voters. By November 1995 mutual fund assets in America totaled more than 2.6 trillion dollars. That's more than Americans have in their savings accounts. In 1990 there were only 3086 mutual funds, by the end of the decade there were more than 7400 mutual funds, which was more than the number of stocks being traded in the major U.S. stock exchanges. In 1996, the cost of trading a stock with Fidelity Investments was $60. By the end of the decade, online trades with Fidelity were under $20. Better still, Ameritrade was asking only $8 per trade.

Today, the clarity of the divisions between Wall Street and Main Street is obscured within the investor class. The socio-economic stratification of Wall Street's investors would evaporate in the 1990s. This was made possible through the day trading craze, the 401k boom, public employee pension funds, and the total democratization of the stock market.

Public Employee Pension Funds

As stated earlier, the average American is heavily invested in the stock market. Many people that are not directly buying securities themselves don't understand that their pensions are tied up in the market. They have no idea of how their money is sometimes being exposed to tremendous risks in how it's being invested; they only know that their jobs are withholding money from their paycheck for their pension. Today, public employee pension funds invest for more than 15 million state, municipal, and educational workers all over America. Their combined assets total more than 3 trillion dollars. The collective power of these shareholders has surpassed that of billionaire heads of corporations, and quite often are the cause of defeat for their proposed policies. The managing CEOs of these pension funds are now assessed on the basis of how much money they can make for their "little guy" clients. Because of their success, many of these managers have become the most powerful men in their state, and leading contending candidates for governor, mayor, or some other high office in government.

The Retirement Systems of Alabama (RSA), is a $25 billion basket of funds invested for 300,000 Alabama public employees—teachers and civil servants. Its director, Dr. David Bronner, has successfully guided these funds into creative as well as conservative securities, and has significantly fueled leveraged buy-outs. He has made teachers and secretaries the new landlords of some of the most recognizable real estate in the world—like the Chase Manhattan Bank Building at 55 Water Street in New York—numerous state of the art golf resorts, and a large new share of corporate America.

Beginning in 1993, Carl McCall became the New York Democratic Party's strongest African American up-and-coming politician, and has been in charge of the second largest public pension fund in America, the New York State Common Retirement Fund (NYSCRF). This fund controls the investments of over 1 million active and retired members. Their collective assets total more than $115 billion. The fund holds about 1.2 million shares of Texaco stock, worth $114 million, which made McCall the true African-American force behind the settlement in the $156 million Racial Discrimination law suits brought against Texaco in 1996-97. Mr. McCall has proven to be a well-heeled success in earning capital gains from leveraged buyouts with pension fund money. As well, Mr. McCall has made significant progress in helping to involve minority owned investment firms—like Blaylock & Partners,

Utendahl Capital Partners, Muriel Siebert & Co. and Samuel A. Ramirez & Co.—into the wealth of the democratized Wall Street of the 1990s.

The largest public pension fund in the United States is the California Public Employees Retirement System (CALPERS). It boasts assets totaling more than $155 billion. CALPERS alone accounts for more than $20 billion of California's economy. The shareholders own more than $8.9 billion in stocks of California based companies. It also holds more than $4.2 billion in mortgages in the state of California.

The impact of these public pension funds on the U.S. economy and corporate shareholder democracy has been astounding. The fuel of their investments in the area of leveraged buyouts along with the volatility of global capital involved in the markets of the 1990s has drastically changed the physiology of corporate America. It has given the little guy a voice, and at the same time, increased the scope and size of a highly unstable market in the global era.

It is frightening to me when I consider the reality that these funds, which make up the retirement savings of Americans, are at significant risk due to the state of our market's fragility and volatility because of the mammoth problem of transient stateless capital. I fear that should 1929 repeat itself, these public pension funds as well as union pension funds could end up being one of the delivery devices which will transfer the aggregated wealth of the poor into the coffers of privately owned central banks, and the corrupt members of the corporate class that have grown up in its shadows.

The Creation of the Financial News Media

In order to educate and entice the public into plowing their savings into the market, which was previously viewed by the average American until the end of the 1980s as the foreign territory of plutocrats, the financial television networks went into high gear with a revamped lineup of news and talk shows. And the people listened. In 1989 almost nobody knew what in the hell CNBC was; it started almost unnoticed on the Nielsen meters. By 1995 CNBC captured more than 55 million homes and profited more than $40 million in the United States. Today with CNBC Asia and CNBC Europe capitalizing on a growing global market, they collectively reach more than 147 million homes in 70 countries. In 1996, Ted Turner's CNN-fn debuted. Along with it came Michael Bloomberg's Bloomberg Television. Today these three are a large part of the world TV diet. In November 1999, CNBC's daytime Nielsen ratings exceeded CNN's.

The 1990s bull market also enabled a huge boom in the financial print media, beginning in 1990 with Time Warner's "Money." Then, Fidelity Investments was born. Worth emerged, followed by Smart Money, backed by Dow Jones in 1992. Today there are too many more to count. Never before in the history of the U.S. has the financial media targeted the average American so aggressively, allowing Wall Street to proselytize the little neophyte capitalists.

Wall Street and the Political Factor

The crescendo of economic growth in the 1990s allowed a Democrat to win two terms in the White House for the first time since 1936. In a transcript of the first TV debate among Bush, Clinton, and Perot on October 12, 1992 in the *New York Times*, Clinton was asked: *"Governor Clinton, when a president running for office for the first time gets into office and wants to do something about the economy, he finds in Washington there's a person who has much more power over the economy than he does: the chairman of the Federal*

Reserve Board, accountable to no one. That being the case, would you go along with proposals made by Treasury Secretary Brady and Congressman Lee Hamilton to make the Federal Reserve Board chairman somehow more accountable to elected officials?" After pausing Clinton responded: *"Well, let me say that I think that we ought to review the terms and the way it works, but frankly, I don't think that's the problem today. We have low interest rates today."* Clinton was smart enough to let Bush take the blame for the recessionary economy during his tenure and fortunate enough to be credited for the economic growth during his time in the White House.

The annual federal budget moved from a $292 billion deficit in 1992 to a $77 billion annual surplus in 1999. There was a massive shift of Wall Street's historical base from Republicans to Democrats. But keep in mind, central bankers like all other international financiers, are in business to make money, historically, without regard to political party agenda. Therefore, regardless of which political party controls government, the agenda of the Federal Reserve, and thereby Wall Street, will always be served. The alignment of White House policy with the initiatives of Wall Street, the Securities & Exchange Commission (SEC), and the Federal Reserve, was the Clinton plan, as advised by Alan Greenspan. It was a method to create another boom cycle by providing incentives to induce the largest expansion of public investment on Wall Street in U.S. history. It also included paying down the national debt, which takes up 50% of the budget, while raising taxes on the wealthiest members of society. In this way, not only does America's private central bankers collect their interest, the Stock Market is once again bursting at the seams with money which, as the 1920s and 30s have taught us, could easily be transferred into the hands of the architects of another shakedown.

In the beginning of his administration, it appeared that the proposed policies of the Bush II administration, in spite of his publicly perceived partisan policy departure from the initiatives of the Clinton administration, have received Greenspan's blessings as well. On January 26, 2001, *The South Florida Sun-Sentinel* newspaper's headline read *"Fed chief embraces tax cuts."* Federal Reserve chairman Alan Greenspan was recorded as saying: *"Should current economic weakness spread beyond what now appears likely, having a tax cut in place may, in fact, do noticeable good."*

Today, in 2004, we see that the tax cut policy of President George W. Bush is the greatest budgetary contributor to the national debt of the Bush tenure. Republicans tell us that deficits are unavoidable because of the war on terror. Are they right? As long as President Bush is able to rally support for unilateralism with vitriolic policies of "going it alone" in the war on terror, deficits will certainly continue to help destroy our prosperity. Dubya inherited a $281 billion surplus, and thanks to "going it alone," in 3 years created a $500 billion deficit. *The Center on Budget and Policy Priorities* called this: *"the largest budgetary meltdown since 1982".* Now, the ten year projection of a $5.6 trillion surplus has fallen by 94% to a reduction of $5.3 trillion; that's $5.3 trillion of our money gone. Dubya forced Congress into raising the debt ceiling by $750 billion. His projected yearly raids on Social Security Fund until the year 2012 to the tune of $1.97 trillion will mean no retirement for baby boomers. But if you only blame the war on terrorism for the deficit, remember, total spending on the war would take almost 70 years to equal the amount spent on Dubya's tax cuts for ten years. As long as Dubya's tax cuts are deficit financed, according to the Brookings Institute: *"the weight of professional opinion suggests they will not lead to higher growth ... a wide range of experts, conclude that we cannot grow our way out of these deficits."*

Dubya called the economy of the 90s *"a binge ... and now we're suffering a hangover."* Begging to differ, I agree

217

with Sen. Hillary Clinton when she said: *"Some have called the Clinton economic record a binge ... Young people being able to afford college, millions climbing out of welfare and into new jobs, and they call that a binge. I'm reminded of what Abraham Lincoln said when some of his commanders complained of U.S. Grant's binges. Find out, he said, what kind of whiskey Grant drinks, because I want to send a barrel to each of my Generals."*

It must be understood that the president of the United States, as well as political leaders of foreign countries, do not control international banking and finance. Those agendas are established, controlled, and coordinated independently by the world's central bankers. Remember, Mayer Rothschild of the Rothschild international banking dynasty in Europe once said: *"Let me control a nation's money and I care not who writes its laws."*

The bottom line—money and the privately owned central banks that create and control it constitute a power that is greater than sovereign governments. The monetary policies of privately owned central banks like the Federal Reserve take precedent over the political process, often times at the expense of politician popular partisan perception. Once again, in other words, when the economy is bad, out go the president and his party. And since central bankers control the economy, the intelligent question is, who really chooses the presidents? In reality no president should be given credit for the status of the economy in America, whether boom or bust. Whatever states and condition the economy is in, it is central bankers who deserve the deepest scrutiny and critique.

Chapter Eleven

The Ideology of Free Market Corporate Liberalism

The Pimp Game

*W*e all are familiar with the image of the American pimp. His big long gaudy Cadillac, the loud clothes and the flashy accouterments became the style in the 1970s. But this was only a front. Though he appeared charming on the outside, hiding on the inside was a shiftless, self-centered, ravenous wolf. He was callous, inconsiderate, and often very cruel to his women working on the street. He never paid taxes, and cheated anyone he caught slipping. He was well protected by shady underworld types, and often times he had corrupt public officials on his pay roll to avoid a trip to the pokey for himself and his employees. When mob pay-offs and political corruption were not expedient, he wouldn't hesitate to take matters into his own hands, and bust a cap in any John's behind that would dare crawfish a trick. His justification for his harsh business ethic was simply: *"It's the nature of the game, baby, nothing personal."* Now most descent people in the 1970s despised pimps. They understood the degradation that pimps brought to their neighborhoods. Most descent parents would never approve of their children becoming pimps or prostitutes. Then why do we accept being pimped by our leaders as they facilitate the dark side of free market corporate capitalism?

There have been far too many debates wherein representatives of rich nations hide behind tired old complaints about population explosions of developing nations in Africa, Asia, Latin America, the Caribbean, and throughout the third world. But the real problem is when we industrialized giants of the west condemn these so-called population explosions within the poor and developing nations of the world; we never address our own over-consumption and the shameful inequity of resource allocation. Like a pimp, living large off of the labor, endangerment, and ignorance of his prostitutes, the free-market corporate capitalism model, which has now emerged as the central economic organizing dynamic of the New World Order, is pimping us all.

Nevertheless, these problems are inseparably linked; consumption, population, and inequity must be dealt with on a collective or global basis. When we stop for a minute and take a look at what's really going on, then we'll see how aspects of these problems have a direct concentrated cause and effect dynamic upon each other. When we open our eyes and see ourselves, or more correctly, see our transnational corporate influence the way our neighbors see it, then we'll see how the industrialized nations of the west have become likened unto pimps under the free market environment of the New World Order. We must understand that we too are not and cannot remain immune to problems of our developing neighbors. Indeed when their economies catch a cold, we start sneezing.

When they starve, we lose weight. When crime rises in their countries because of unemployment, we had better lock our doors. When drugs flow from their countries as their main export, we become inebriated and our society is compromised.

The First and Second Principles of Free Market Ideology

World markets are currently under assault by the principles of the new free market corporate ideology. To get a clear understanding of the dynamics of this assault, we must examine what these principles say. In his book, **"When Corporations Rule the World,"** Dr. David Korten said the first principle claims: *"Sustained economic growth, as measured by Gross National Product, is the best path to human progress."* In other words, we measure progress in our society by how much money we earn collectively as a nation.

It is my contention that *"sustained economic growth,"* (judged only by the measurement of GNP statistics, touted as being *"the best path to human progress"*), is a pipe dream for the working class. The problem with this ideology is that the GNP doesn't measure street business. What do I mean by street business? I mean bartering; GNP doesn't measure that, or much of the huge volume of cash transactions in America. GNP doesn't measure volunteerism, donated services, or any other income, trade, or quality of life enhancement that does not register on the government's tax radar screens.

The GNP is not an accurate socio-economic measurement, period. The shift from social measurements to monetary measurements (the GNP) makes society more dependent upon those who have assets, major capital, and control of jobs. At the same time, it disannuls and dismantles systems of bartering and service swaps as a sustainable

221

economic model, which has endured for centuries all over the world.

This ideology neglects to honor humanitarianism's meaningful contributions to the greatness of this nation. We must also understand that this type of thinking gives license for the government to cater to the needs of corporations over the needs of the people. The rationale says "what's good for the corporations is ultimately good for the people," but the historical reality has been "what's good for the corporations is usually bad for the people." NAFTA has been good for corporations, but bad for the working class.

Furthermore, environmental ramifications within developing nations are catastrophic because of the second principle of free-market corporate capitalism, which, according to Korten, says that: *"Free markets, unrestrained by governments, generally result in the most efficient and socially optimal allocation of resources."* This is historically not the case. First let me deal with how the depletion of resources affects the poor. When natural resources are depleted, corporations make profits, but peasants, whose livelihood is vitally dependent upon these resources, are displaced and dispossessed. The environmental ramifications of rain forest deforestation on farmers and fishermen, and the subsequent rise in crime, alcoholism, drug abuse, and suicide, are prime examples of what happens when our corporations move into a country, solely for profit. In the privatization of China's agricultural industrial complex, thousands have been dispossessed. Secondly, throughout the history of the modern world, wealth has always been transferred from one class of citizens to another. This isn't by accident. So the question is, which social group will receive the most optimal allocation of resources?

The Third Principle of Free Market Ideology

Dr. Korten also tells us that the third principle of free market corporate capitalism says: *"Economic globalization, achieved by removing barriers to the free flow of goods and money anywhere in the world, increased competition, economic efficiency, creates jobs, lowers consumer prices, increases consumer choice, increases economic growth, and is generally beneficial to everyone."*

First let's look at the assumption of the *"free flow of goods."* US subsides within developing nations grossly imbalance trade in corporate America's favor, inhibiting the equitable flow of goods, except in countries designated for industrialization, such as China, who has enjoyed a 26 to 1 trade imbalance with the US.

Second let's look at *"increased competition."* American workers now compete with cheap labor from abroad. The H-1B Job Training Program, favored by President Bush, allows foreign workers to take American jobs. In addition to that, NAFTA and the FTAA are rapidly de-industrializing America as well. In an article in the **New York Times** by Charles Schumer and Paul Craig Roberts called, **"Second Thoughts on Free Trade,"** an important aspect of labor dynamics is assessed: *"We are concerned that the United States may be entering a new economic era in which American workers will face direct global competition at almost every job level—from the machinist to the software engineer to the Wall Street analyst. Any worker whose job does not require daily face-to-face interaction is now in jeopardy of being replaced by a lower-paid, equally skilled worker thousands of miles away."*

Third let's look at *"economic efficiency."* Ad hoc trade regulations and corporate profit motives are implemented without regard for economic and environmental ramifications. Example: Florida's sugar growers' victory over recently proposed amendments to establish a sugar production tax has shifted the costly burden of Everglades restoration to the public. Floridians will now suffer future tax increases and environmental compromises in the name of free market "economic efficiency."

Fourth let's look at *"job creation."* Because labor costs are extremely low in developing nations, most jobs are being created abroad, at the expense of record job losses within America. Again in the **New York Times** article by Charles Schumer and Paul Craig Roberts, the authors tell us that *"American jobs are being lost not to competition from foreign companies, but to multinational corporations, often with American roots, that are cutting costs by shifting operations to low-wage countries."*

Fifth let's look at *"lower consumer prices."* Markets in developing nations can't support the products produced by their host western manufacturers. Neither are they equipped to handle all the other associated tumultuous economic ramifications associated with hosting western corporations (consolidation, displacement, IMF structural adjustments, WTO initiatives, etc ...). Therefore prices fall because of decreased demand within their core markets, and the deflation is exported to us. Thus "lower consumer prices" are created at the expense of deflation. Imported deflation into the U. S. not only compromises price optimization, it also causes corporations to reduce labor costs in an attempt to reconcile their debts. In an article in the Economist magazine, October 10, 2002, entitled, **"Of Debt, Deflation, and Denial,"** the danger of deflation to this country is described: *"America's corporate sector is already suffering deflation, with the price deflator of non-financial businesses falling in the past year for the first time* *since the Second World War. Many firms that borrowed heavily in the late 1990s, expecting rapid revenue growth to finance their debts, are now in trouble. Ed McKelvey, an economist at Goldman Sachs, worries that corporate-sector deflation could create wider deflation if firms try to slash labour costs."*

Sixth let's look at *"increased consumer choice."* Yes, they've given us a wider variety of choices of foreign produced goods. So wide that we have become the largest consumption basket on earth, while producing next to nothing. How long do you think we can continue like that? Not only that; a growing number of Americans are increasingly concerned about the near slave labor conditions that these products are produced under in foreign countries. A US News & World Report article on December 16, 1996 entitled, ***"Economic Justice in the Market Place,"*** said: *"A US News poll shows that 6 in 10 Americans are concerned about the working conditions under which products are made in the United States and more than 9 in 10 are concerned about the working conditions under which products are made in Asia and Latin America."*

Seventh, the *"economic growth"* they refer to is global in scope. Because international trade in today's open free market environment is still conducted under the old "closed market regulations," stable economic growth is impossible. You must have rules which apply to the game. You can't play football under basketball rules. That's why the new global free market ideology has created a completely unstable transnational economic environment. The AFL-CIO, in an article posted on their website entitled, ***"New Rules for the Global Economy,"*** said: *"If we do not fundamentally change U.S. policies and the policies of the international institutions in which the U.S. government plays such an important role, we will continue to lose good jobs, our trade deficit will continue to soar, inequality will continue to grow, corporate power will* *become more concentrated and the world's poorest nations will fall further behind. The American people will—and should—reject a policy of global engagement that comes with these costs ... The current framework of global rules has failed miserably on many crucial counts. The international financial system has promoted policies that left many developing countries vulnerable and unprepared in the face of currency volatility and unpredictable swings in speculative capital flows. The result was thousands of bankruptcies and suicides and tens of millions of people losing their livelihood and falling into desperate poverty. The international financial institutions pressured crisis countries to export their way out of their problems—exacerbating deindustrialization and a rising trade deficit in the United States."*

Lastly but not least, in the New World Order, the prime beneficiaries of free market capitalism are banks and the corporations that grow up around them. The bottom line, up to now free market capitalism has helped create unemployment, economic instability, destruction of nationalistic economic sovereignty, and it breeds anti-American sentiments abroad. In an article by Dean Baker called, ***"From New Economy to War Economy,"*** in ***Dollars and Sense Magazine***, the author tells us: *"... if the United States wants to avoid being the target of future acts of terrorism, it should try doing some good in the world. More than 35 million people in the developing world are HIV positive. The United States pledged $200 million—six hours of the Pentagon's budget—to address the problem. At the same time, it threatens trade sanctions against countries that provide low-cost <u>drugs</u> by ignoring the patents of U.S. pharmaceutical companies."*

The Fourth Principle of Free Market Ideology

Dr. Korten also tells us that the fourth principle of free market corporate capitalism says: *"Privatization, which moves*

226

the functions of governments, and assets of governments, from governments themselves to the private sector, increases efficiency, reduces prices, increases responsiveness to consumer preferences." The problem with that ideology is, when unregulated, private industry operates under a strict profit motive without regard for America's nationalistic sovereignty, the working class, or the environment. It encourages corporations to lay off their workers, or outsource labor outside of the United States. That's the kind of *"responsiveness"* that privatization under the free-market ideology demonstrates to America. According to an article in the Wall Street journal entitled, ***"Bush Officials Draft Broad Plan for Free Market Economy in Iraq,"*** by Neil King Jr., it seems the Bush administration is planning to prescribe privatization for the post-Saddam economy in Iraq: *"The Bush administration has drafted sweeping plans to remake Iraq's economy in the U.S. image. Hoping to establish a free-market economy in Iraq following the fall of Saddam Hussein, the U.S. is calling for the privatization of state-owned industries such as parts of the oil sector, forming a stock market complete with electronic trading and fundamental tax reform."* The Bush administration still insists, "It's not about oil." Let's continue to examine other aspects of this ideology.

As far as *"increased efficiency"* is concerned, all I can see is that it's economically more efficient for corporations to pay a non-unionized foreign employee the small fraction of what they have to pay Americans. In the case of developing nations, according to the **Wikipedia Free Encyclopedia**, privatization can decrease economic efficiency because *"where free-market economics are rapidly imposed, a country may not have the bureaucratic tools necessary to regulate it."*

"Reduced prices" is often the result of deflation. One major negative aspect of deflation occurs when corporations are forced to reduce prices to the point that their profits are

227

compromised; their immediate solution is to reduce their workforce. Unfortunately, in a racist society such as ours, that generally means that minorities are the first to go. Eventually, the working class is forced to take up the slack during the erosion of the tax base as corporations outsource labor abroad.

Dr. Korten further indicates several underlying assumptions of the free market ideology that he says are *"based on the negative aspects of our nature,"* which assumes that humans are motivated by self interest, and the quest for financial gain. In other words, free market proponents want us to believe that people by nature are only motivated by greed. That's garbage!

Another assumption is that the *"action that yields the greatest financial gain for the individual or firm also yields the most benefit to society."* In other words, a rising tide lifts all boats. Caution: sometimes the smaller boats get smashed upon the rocks and destroyed. Again, according to the **Wikipedia Free Encyclopedia**, *"Profits from successful enterprises end up in private pockets instead of being available for the common good."*

Another stone in this temple of free market greed is the assumption that *"competitive behavior is more rational to the individual than cooperative behavior, and ultimately more beneficial for society."* In other words, the drive to acquire physical wealth is the highest expression of what it means to be human. More garbage! Unbridled avarice is not a positive attribute. The relentless pursuit of greed has not led to socially optimal outcomes for society, only a greater stratification between rich and poor, which further compromises national security and democracy itself. A classic example of the disaffection engendered by the free market proponent's relentless pursuit of greed was seen when the Associated Press reported mass anti-globalism protests in South Africa as follows: *"JOHANNESBURG, South Africa, Aug 31, 2002 (AP World Stream via) COMTEX)—About 10,000 protesters marched from a sprawling township of tin shacks and open sewers Saturday to the U.N. World Summit, demanding leaders do more to fight poverty and save the planet ... 'What is this summit doing for us? It is providing for the rich, not the poor,' said Mathius Ledwaba, who had a sign stuck in his cap reading, 'Submarines, fighting jets, machine guns won't fight unemployment and HIV/AIDS.'"'*

Finally Korten tells us this ideology suggests that *"human progress and improvements in well being are best measured in the aggregate market value of output."* As we have previously discussed, the government's measurement of the aggregate market value of our collective productivity, called the gross domestic output or GDP, doesn't measure unreported bartering, volunteerism, and cash transactions—street business.

Bottom line: historically, the interests of the working class are not and have not been best served by encouraging, honoring, and rewarding these selfish principles.

The Corporate Libertarian Alliance

Free market proponents seek justification for greed and selfishness by twisting fair economic principles that once made America great. These insights and ideas are so deeply embedded that now they are unquestioned, accepted, and incorporated into public policy.

Neo-liberal economists tell us that the free market is our "manifest destiny." Those who can't or refuse to adapt will be run over. These people refuse to advocate or develop a more democratically framed system. Instead, this ideology is sanitized by an alliance of misguided and bought-off free market economists, property rights advocates, and corporate class individuals, together advancing the free market ideology. Korten refers to these proponents as the *"corporate libertarian alliance."*

Corporate libertarian property rights advocates, according to Dr. Korten, *"are only interested in protecting the interests of large property owners over the public interest."* Those without property, in their eyes, have no rights that property rights advocates are bound to respect. According to Roger Pilon of the Cato Institute, *"Indeed, despotic governments have long understood that if you control property, you control the media, the churches, the political process itself."* Again, as with corporate libertarian economists, property rights advocates like the Cato Institute, who promote this type of ideology, are rewarded by corporations through political empowerment and big money.

The *"corporate class"* consists of corporate managers, lawyers, consultants, PR specialists, brokers, and investors. These individuals, Korten says, *"make up the third pillar of the corporate libertarian alliance."* To me they appear to have no conscience, no moral compass, no compassion, and no sense of nationalism, patriotism, or humanism. To them, the devastating democratic, social, and environmental ramifications of their actions are justified purely by the satisfaction of their greed. They have a heady and high minded kind of intellectual and class prejudice. They also have a demonic alliance and myopic service to the New World Order agenda.

But what is the ultimate reward for selling your soul to the corporate New World Order? In the corporate class dynamic, everyone is expendable, as corporations are taking on a rambunctious life of their own. Dr. Korten said: *"The enormous political success of the alliance in shielding corporations from public accountability has created a monster that even the corporate class no longer controls and is creating a world they would scarcely wish to bequeath to their children."* President Abraham Lincoln adds: *"The money power preys upon the nation in times of peace and conspires against it in times of adversity. It is more despotic than monarchy, more insolent than autocracy, more selfish than bureaucracy. I see in the near future a crisis approaching that unnerves me and causes me to tremble for the safety of my country. Corporations have been enthroned, an era of corruption will follow, and the money power of the country will endeavor to prolong its reign by working upon the prejudices of the people, until the wealth is aggregated in a few hands, and the republic destroyed."*

In the final analysis, corporations rule the world, and no longer governments (we the people).

Adam Smith on Principles of the Fair Market

Free market proponents claim the 18th century economist Adam Smith as their patron saint. But their ideology would likely not meet the approval of Smith today. The free market ideology opposes restraint on corporate size and power. Smith on the other hand, in his book *"The Wealth of the Nations,"* written in 1776, opposed any form of economic monopoly on the grounds that it *"distorts the market's natural ability to establish a price that provides a fair return on land, labor and capital; to produce a satisfactory outcome for both buyers and sellers; and to optimally allocate society's resources."*

Most trade agreements of contemporary corporate liberalism seek protectionism or exclusive ownership of intellectual property rights for corporations through their agents in governments. Smith was strongly opposed to "trade secrets" as *"contrary to fair market principles."* The spirit of Smith's work leads me to conclude that he would have opposed protectionism, exclusivity, and the associated price-gouging of a monopoly, especially on such things as a life saving drug, because of the benefits to all humanity. Recently, President Bush and Bill Gates found out that Nelson Mandela also opposes that type of price gouging when they offered badly needed AIDS-fighting pharmaceuticals to South Africa at seven times the price offered by competing countries. We must learn; sometimes actual circumstances of human reality are totally different than theoretical economics.

Yes, Smith's work was an economic blue-print during a time when America's economy was largely agricultural, not the highly industrial and technologically driven economy of today. Yes, Smith advocated getting the highest price (price optimization) for a farmer trying to get top dollar for his crops; that's self-interest. But he did not intend to provide the type of protectionism for corporate elites which allow a CEO to lay-off 10,000 workers while paying himself millions.

The free market ideology encourages the existence of cartels, monopolies, and eradication of competition, to control prices and maximize profits. Smith, on the other hand, encouraged competition within markets to ensure prices favorable to the consumer. What we have in America today is far from what Smith envisioned. Example: How can the thousands of small wheat farmers compete with the "Big 4" wheat producers—Conagra, ADM Milling, Cargill, and Pillsbury, who together produce more than 60% of the world's wheat?

Adam Smith's single paragraph, out of 1000 pages in *"The Wealth of Nations"* about *"protected markets"* translating self-interests into benefits for the general society, cannot be applied to today's "global environment." Indeed, the principle of a rising tide within protected and isolated markets lifting all boats assumes that, as in Smith's time, the investments of the entrepreneur would remain local where a small local economy can universally prosper from those investments. Travel by air, faxes, email, the internet, and global banking institutions didn't exist during Smith's time to facilitate the de-industrialization of nations and the associated economic hardships for the working class.

CONCLUSION

Inductive reasoning will lead the average person in America today to conclude that because U.S. citizens and businesses own stock in companies all over the world and people all over the world own stock in companies in the U.S. there must be a global banking system. After all America, being the "land of opportunity," was built with immigrant money from all over the world. Besides, the rights to own property, invest, and engage in business are guaranteed in this country.

Sounds good and it's true to an extent. However we must understand that when these rights were framed within the Constitution our money was backed by gold and taxes were almost zero in the United States. And most importantly, the authors of that document never intended for money and credit in the United States to be controlled by privately owned central banks. They never intended for these institutions to plunder and make debt slaves of future Americans.

Throughout the long history of failed experiments with privately owned central banks the recurring theme of their tenure has been the debauchery of currency through the principle of dishonest weights and measures (Deut.25:13-15), perpetually expanding debt and inflation, as well as economic recession and depression. Not to mention war and its associated hardships on society. Now even the cautious Alan Greenspan, chairman of the Fed, after a three and a half year long cheap-money policy, has finally conceded that President Bush's tax cuts came at a fortuitous time for the economy. Its been almost three years since the recession is said to have ended, and economic growth in the United States is still very sluggish. The uncertain nature of the recovery, coupled with fears about gas prices, irrational exuberance in the stock market, the specter of terrorism, and the war in Iraq have all prompted 13 interest rate cuts since January 2001 in an attempt to bolster America's critically anemic economy, without positive results.

The main problem is debt, systematically created, mainly by massive tax cuts for the rich, a very large re-organization and expansion of the federal government on an unprecedented scale, and Fed bailouts. The resulting mammoth expansion of the currency supply because of these policies has finally taken its toll on this economy. This nation, her businesses, and individuals can't see the light of day because of their debt. The greatest burden to America and the world is the insurmountable burden of debt. Thanks to the unconstitutional imposition of a 4th privately owned central bank in America, this nation's money supply now totals approximately 4 trillion dollars in inconvertible, irredeemable, intrinsically worthless, and inflationary FEDERAL RESERVE NOTES. But our national debt totals more than 14 trillion. With a debt to asset ratio like this the scales can never be balanced, leaving America on the verge of foreclosure. Historically, debt has been the cause of the demise of marriages, businesses, and empires. Remember, the book of Proverbs says: *"The rich ruleth over the poor, and the borrower is servant to the lender."* (Proverb 22:7)

Hopefully the reader can now see that America's economic chaos, enslavement, and global capital dilemma was caused by abandoning principles of fairness and honesty in favor of the dishonest methods used by central bankers. (Lam.5:1-15) The stock market crash of 1987, the further loss of economic sovereignty through so-called "free trade" agreements like NAFTA and FTAA, are undisputedly the result of central banker policy. They control how much your mortgage payments are and whether or not you have a job.

They are the architects of the New World order. They are the rulers of the world.

When JFK said In his inaugural address: *"And yet the same revolutionary beliefs for which our forbears fought are still at issue around the globe ... the belief that the rights of man come not from the generosity of the state but from the hand of God. We dare not forget today that we are the heirs of that first revolution,"* he was correlating the class based economic servitude in Europe and the American colonies with the same class based economic order today. In his book *"Jefferson's Pillow,"* author Roger Wilkins points out the agenda of the late 17th century ruling class elite through their London policy maker puppets: *"People who were viewed as idle, dangerous, or too undisciplined were targeted for export to the New World, where they would be put to work making money for the mother country. They were for the most part indentured servants, owned usually for seven year terms, during which time they could be bought and sold."* In other words until 1676 some whites, and until 1863 nearly all blacks, lived in slavery to support a cruel economic system, which benefited only the rich. White and Black revolutionaries under the leadership of Nathaniel Bacon revolted and burned and plundered the Jamestown homes of the wealthiest Virginians, bringing an end to the most oppressive aspects of the economic servitude of whites in the summer of 1676. Blacks would have to wait for almost 200 years.

Slavery still exists in America today—economic slavery. The gap between the rich and poor in this country is growing wider and wider. The middle class is rapidly disappearing because of the erosion of their purchasing power due to the dollar crisis. They are under assault by greedy corporations that are stealing their jobs and their pensions. One only needs to look at the tremendous earning gap between CEOs at the top and their workers near the bottom of the totem pole to begin to wonder if the notion of a middle class is a joke. In her book *"Pigs at the Trough"*, Arianna Huffington tells us just how greedy CEOs have become: *"Former Kmart CEO Charles Conaway received nearly $23 million in compensation during his two-year tenure. When Kmart filed for bankruptcy in 2002, 283 stores were closed and 22,000 employees lost their jobs. None of them received any severance pay whatsoever.*

"Former Tyco CEO Dennis Kozlowski made nearly $467 million in salary, bonuses and stock during his four year tenure. Shareholders lost a massive $92 billion when Tyco's market value plunged.

"The CEOs of 23 large companies under investigation by the SEC and other agencies earned 70% more than the average CEO, banking a collective $1.4 billion between 1999 and 2001. Since January 2001 the market value of these 23 companies nosedived by over $500 billion, or roughly 73%, and they laid off over 160,000 employees.

"In the year before Enron collapsed, about 100 executives and energy traders collected more than $300 million in cash payments from the company. More than $100 million went to former CEO Kenneth Lay. After filing for bankruptcy, Enron lost $68 billion in market value, 5,000 employees lost their jobs, and Enron workers lost $800 million from their pension funds.

"Wal-Mart CEO H. Lee Scott, Jr. received more than $1.7 million in total compensation in 2001. Wal-Mart employees in 30 states are suing the company alleging that managers forced employees to punch out after an eight-hour work day, and then continue working for no pay. This is a clear violation of the Fair Labor Standards Act, which says employees who

work more than 40 hours a week must be paid time and a half for their overtime.

"The richest 20% of Americans earn almost 50% of the nation's income. The poorest 20% of Americans earn 5.2%.

"The top 1% of stock owners hold 47.7% of all stocks by value. The bottom 80% of stock owners own just 4.1% of total stock holdings.

"In 2000, the average CEO earned more in one day than the average worker earned all year. In 2000, 25% of workers earned less than poverty level wages.

Between 1990 and 2000, average CEO pay rose 571%. Between 1990 and 2000, average worker pay rose 37%."

Arianna's book is a must read. If what she has to say does not convince most white people in this country that the working class is under assault nothing will. Black people and women have always been under assault in America. This is the unfortunate reason behind the civil unrest and riots by black people in this country. But the government has shown that it has a serious plan to deal with a population in unrest during times of peace. Anytime there is an uprising of the people in America because of the oppressive economic policies of the Federal Reserve, a carefully planned action of containment, and if necessary, extermination is implemented by the U.S. government on behalf of the international bankers. Programs like J. Edgar Hoover's COINTELPRO (counter-intelligence program) of the 1960s are implemented to overthrow so-called dissident and revolutionary movements in America, by any and all means necessary. Likewise, during this time, the government continued its quest of controlling the American people and their rebellions, through ideas from a study called the

"Report from Iron Mountain." The report concluded that, in the past, war was the only way to control the people. But under a one world government, war is unlikely. Therefore it was through the "Report from Iron Mountain" that new methods of maintaining social and civil order were devised. A part of the report is quoted as follows:

"We will examine ... the time honored use of military institutions to provide anti-social elements with an acceptable role in social structure ... In earlier days these conditions were dealt with directly by the military without the complications of due process, usually through press gangs or outright enslavement ....

"Most proposals that address themselves, explicitly or otherwise to the postwar problem of controlling the socially alienated turn to some variant of the Peace Corps or the so-called Job Corps for a solution. The socially disaffected, the economically unprepared, the psychologically uncomfortable, the hard core delinquents, the incorrigible subversives, and the rest of the unemployable are seen as somehow transformed by the disciplines of a service modeled on military precedent into more or less dedicated social service workers....

"Another possible surrogate for the control of potential enemies of society is the reintroduction, in some form consistent with modern technology and political process, of slavery.... It is entirely possible that the development of a sophisticated form of slavery may be an absolute prerequisite for social control in a world at peace ...." With exclusive control of interest rates, the graduated income tax, influence over the FBI and the initiatives of the "Iron Mountain Report," the Federal Reserve has at its disposal, a devastating array of weapons, which it has used, and will use again against the

American middle class. This is nothing short of an economic death decree against the sovereignty of America.

The point that I am making here is Mystery Babylon was cast down in that instance, along with every time men have been oppressed, through the principles of dishonesty and greed. I see Mystery Babylon as our current economic, political, and ecclesiastical system. If the bible is right, it must ultimately be cast down. (Rev.18th Ch) The entire system is based on DEBT. If everyone—government and citizen—could resist the lust of our eyes, the temptation to borrow, and simply live within our means, the system could not survive. But how this system will meet its ultimate demise once and for all is still unknown. It rests only in the hands of the architect of heaven and earth.

Bibliography

Introduction

Quigley, Carroll. (1966) *Tragedy and Hope.* New York, Macmillan Company.

Solomon, Steve. (1995) *The Confidence Game.* New York, Simon & Schuster.

Chapter One

Coogan, Gertrude. (1935). *Money Creators.* New York: Sound Money Press, Inc.

Griffin, G. Edward. (1994) *The Creature from Jekyll Island.* Westlake, Ca.: American Media. pg. 6

Mullins, Eustace. (1993) *The Secrets of the Federal Reserve.* Clackamas, Or.: Emissary Publications.

O'Neill, Paul. (2004) *The Price of Loyalty.* New York: Simon & Schuster.

Patman, Hon. Wright (1977), the Late Vice Chairman of the Joint Economic Committee, *The Federal Reserve System: A Study Prepared for the Use of the Joint Economic Committee, Congress of the United States.* Appendix I. Law Review Articles of Wright Patman. pg. 145

Paul, Congressman Ron. (2002) *U.S. House of Representatives.*

Smith, Vera C. (1981) *The Rationale of Central Banking.* Committee For Monetary Research and Education.

Chapter Two

Carmack, Patrick and Still, Bill. (1996) *The Money Masters*, Still Productions.

Galbraith, John (1995) *Money: Whence It Came, Where It Went.* Houghton Mifflin Co.

Greider, William (1987) *Secrets of the Temple.* New York: Touchstone/Simon & Schuster.

Griffin, G. Edward. (1994) *The Creature from Jekyll Island.* Westlake, Ca.: American Media.

Mullins, Eustace. (1993) *The Secrets of the Federal Reserve.* Clackamas, Or.: Emissary Publications.

Chapter Three

Bancroft, George. (1982) *A Plea for the Constitution of the United States.* First published Spencer Judd, Publisher.

Carmack, Patrick and Still, Bill. (1996) *The Money Masters*, Still Productions.

Davis, Gareth. *The Destruction of the Second Bank of the United States Rationale and Effects*, from: http://www.maths.tcd.ie/local/JUNK/econrev/ser/html/destructi on.html.

Franklin, Benjamin. *Quotes from Individuals Who Understood the Dangers of a Privately Created and Controlled Money System*, from http://members.aol.com/crossover2/quotes. htm.

Goodrich, Rev. Charles A. (1856) *Lives of the Signers to the Declaration of Independence.* New York: William Reed & Co. pg. 233-244

Gouge, William M. (1968) *A Short History of Paper Money and Banking in the United States.* New York: Augustus M. Kelley, Publisher.
Griffin, G. Edward. (1994) *The Creature from Jekyll Island.* Westlake, Ca.: American Media.

Kline, Eugene. (1964) *Money and Banking.* Cincinnati, Ohio: South-Western publishing.

Myers, Gustavus. (2002) *The History of Great American Fortunes.* University Press of the Pacific.

Temin, Peter. (1968) *The Economic Consequences of the Bank War.* Journal of Political Economy. pg. 76

Warren, Dr. Lee. *The PLIM Report.* www.plim.org.

Wilson, Derek. (1994) *The Rothschilds.* Andre Deutsch Ltd.

Chapter Four

African-American Perspectives: Pamphlets from the Daniel A. P. Murray Collection 1880-1920. Rare Book and Special Collections Division, Library of Congress.

Allen, Gary. (1976) *The Rockefeller File.* CPA Books.

Basler, Roy P. (1953) *The Collected Works of Abraham Lincoln.* From First Inaugural Address, in Lincoln, Vol. IV., ed. New Brunswick, NJ: Rutgers University Press. pg. 262-271

Brown, Tony. (1999) *Empower the People.* New York: Quill/William Morrow & Company. pg. 140-141

Clark, Thomas J. *The True American Way.* Family Guardian Publications

Griffin, G. Edward. (1994) *The Creature from Jekyll Island.* Westlake, Ca.: American Media. pg. 269
Harper's Weekly. (1910) Vol. 54, Issue 2785.

Humes, James C. (1999) *The Wit and Wisdom of Abraham Lincoln.* Gramercy.

James, Alexander *The History of Money and Private Central Bank Ownership by Freemason/Zionists Mafia.* Portland, Oregon: Portland Independent Media Center.
http://portland.indymedia.org/en/2003/06/266805.shtml.

Kennan, H. S. (1996) *The Federal Reserve Bank.* Los Angeles: Noontime Press.

Kolko, Gabriel. (1977) *The Triumph of Conservatism.* Reissue Edition, New York: Simon & Schuster, Free Press; a division of the Macmillan Co., 1963.

LaRouche Jr., Lyndon. (1997) *Dope, Inc.*, 3rd Edition. Executive Intelligence Review, Ben Franklin Booksellers.

Lindbergh Sr. Rep. Charles. (1913) *Banking and Currency and the Money Trust.* Washington D.C.: National Capital Press.

Lincoln, Abraham. (1996) *Abraham Lincoln: In His Own Words.* Barnes & Noble Books: Maureen Harrison & Steve Gilbert, Editors.

Lincoln: His Words and His world. Waukesha, Wisconsin: Country Beautiful Foundation, 1965. pg. 54

Lundberg, Ferdinand. *America's Sixty Families.* New York. Pg 221

McAdoo, William. (1931) *Crowded Years.* New York: Houghton Mifflin. Pg. 165-66
Mullins, Eustace. (1993) *The Secrets of the Federal Reserve.* Clackamas, Or.: Emissary Publications.

Palast, Greg. (2004) *Vanishing Votes.* The Observer. London: The Guardian Media Group.

Rothbard, Murray N. (1963) *America's Great Depression.* Kansas City: Sheed and Ward. pg. 101-105

Ruml, Beardsley. (1946) *Taxes for Revenue are Obsolete.* American Affairs. pg. 35

Search, Dr. R. E. (1998) *Lincoln Money Martyred.* CPA Books.

Vennard W. B. *The Federal Reserve Hoax.* Palmdale, CA: Omni Publications.

Viereck, George S. (1932) *The Strangest Friendship in History: Woodrow Wilson and Colonel House.* New York: Liveright Publishers. pg. 4

Woodward, Bob. (2004) *Plan of Attack.* New York: Simon & Schuster.

Chapter Five

Allen, Gary. (1990) *None Dare Call It Conspiracy.* Buccaneer Books.

Churchill, Winston. (1949) *The World Crisis*. New York: Scribner's Sons. pg. 300. (1993) Barnes & Nobles. pg. 464

Epperson, A. Ralph. (1990) *The Unseen Hand*. Tucson, Arizona: Publius Press. pg. 100
Espionage History 1917-1918. Page Wise, Inc., Publisher. http://ncnc.essortment.com/ espionagehistor_rago.htm.

Ferrell, Robert. (1985) *Woodrow Wilson and World War*. New York: Harpers and Row. pg. 35

Finder, Joseph (1983) *Red Carpet*. New York: Holt, Reinhart, & Winston. pg. 8

Griffin, G. Edward. (1994) *The Creature from Jekyll Island*. Westlake, Ca.: American Media. pg. 6

Katkov, George. (1967) *Russia 1917: The February Revolution*. New York: Harper & Row.

McAdoo, William. (1931) *Crowded Years*. New York: Houghton Mifflin. pg. 392

Seymour, Charles (1926) *The Intimate Papers of Colonel House*. New York: Houghton Mifflin. pg. 434-435

Sutton, Antony. (1975) *Wall Street and the Bolshevik Revolution*. New Rochelle, New York: Arlington House.

Trotsky, Leon. (1930) *My Life*. New York: Scribner's. pg. 277

Wilson, Woodrow, Bushnell-Hart, Albert, Editor. (2002) *Selected Addresses and the Public Papers of Woodrow Wilson*. University Press of the Pacific.

Chapter Six

Allen, Gary. (1990) *None Dare Call It Conspiracy.* Buccaneer Books.

Arizona Daily Star. September 12, 1980, pg. 10A
Brzezinski, Zbigniew. (1970) *Between two ages; America's Role in the Technetronic Era.* New York: Viking Press.

The Commercial and Financial Chronicle. (1929) pg. 1444

Epperson, A. Ralph. (1990) *The Unseen Hand.* Tucson, Arizona: Publius Press. pg. 241

Griffin, G. Edward. (1994) *The Creature from Jekyll Island.* Westlake, Ca.: American Media. pg. 6

Horowitz, David. (1993) *The Rockefellers: An American Dynasty.* Blackstone Audio Books.

Huffington, Arianna. (2003) *Pigs at the Trough.* New York: Three Rivers Press. pg. 14

James, Alexander. *Portland IMC.*
http://portland.indymedia.org/en/2003/06/266805.shtml.

Marrs, Jim. (2000) *Rule by Secrecy.* Harper Collins Publishers. pg. 31

Wilson, Woodrow, Bushnell-Hart, Albert, Editor. (2002) *Selected Addresses and the Public Papers of Woodrow Wilson.* University Press of the Pacific.

Chapter Seven

Brown, Tony. (1999) *Empower the People.* New York: Quill/William Morrow & Company.

Epperson, A. Ralph. (1990) *The Unseen Hand.* Tucson, Arizona: Publius Press.

Pelley, William Dudley. (1936) *Pelley's Weekly.*

Quigley, Carroll. (1966) *Tragedy and Hope.* New York, Macmillan Company.

Sutton, Antony C. *Wall Street and the Rise of Hitler.* Seal Beach, CA: Hidden Mysteries Books, 76 Press.

Chapter Eight

Chua, Amy. *World on Fire.* (2002) New York: Doubleday.

Global Policy Forum.
http://www.globalpolicy.org/globaliz/econ/.

Griffin, G. Edward. (1994) *The Creature from Jekyll Island.* Westlake, Ca.: American Media. pg. 6

The Internationalist: Business Guide to the World-Mexico, Canada, and Latin America. Boston, Massachusetts: The Internationalist Publishing Company.

Keynes, John Maynard. (1930) *The Collected Writings of John Maynard Keynes Vol. V.* London: Macmillan & Company.

Keynes, John Maynard. *The Economic Consequences of the Peace.* McMaster University Archive for the History of Economic Thought in its series History of Economic Thought Books with number keynes1919.

The King James Version of the Bible.

Moberg, David. (2003) *In These Times.*
http://www.inthesetimes.com/.

Quigley, Carroll. (1966) *Tragedy and Hope.* New York,
Macmillan Company.
Review of the News, The Human Cost of Communism in China.
(1972) U.S. Senate Committee on the Judiciary.

Joseph Stiglitz, (2002) *Globalization and its Discontents.* New
York: W. W. Norton & Company.

Turner, Dennis. (1983) *When Your Bank Fails.* Amwell
Publishing, Inc.

Chapter Nine

Ahlseen, Mark. (1996) *It's Not Nice to Make Money.* Contra
Mundum.
http://www.visi.com/~contram/cm/reviews/cm15_rev_money.html.

Brady, Nicholas. (1987) *Presidential Task Force on Market
Mechanisms.* U. S. Treasury Department.

Choate, Pat. (1991) *Agents of Influence.* Touchstone Edition.
New York: Simon & Schuster.

Ducker, Peter. (1986) *The Changed World Economy.* Foreign
Affairs.

Gross, Daniel, (2000) *Bull Run.* New York: Public Affair
Publishing/Perseus Book Group.

Macrae, Norman. (1990) *The Economist.*

Reich, Cary. (1989) *Institutional Investor Magazine.*
"The Privatization of Paul Volcker."

Snellgrove, Don. *Concord Forex Group*. www.cfgtrading.com.
Solomon, Steven. (1995) *The Confidence Game*. New York,
Simon & Schuster.

Stevenson, Merril. *A Game of Skill As Well: Survey of
International Banking*. The Economist.

The Wall Street Journal. (1988).

Chapter Ten

The Center on Budget and Policy Priorities. Washington, DC.
http://www.cbpp.org/

The South Florida Sun-Sentinel. (2001) Ft. Lauderdale, Fl.

Gross, Daniel, (2000) *Bull Run*. New York: Public Affair
Publishing/Perseus Book Group.

Chapter Eleven

Baker, Dean. (2001) *From New Economy to War Economy*.
Dollars and Sense, Cambridge, Maryland.

Feldman, Fred. (2002) *10,000 march against privatization, for
Palestine at Johannesburg world summit*. Associated Press.
Sun. 01 Sept. 2002, 16:48 GMT

Economic Justice in the Market Place. (1996) US News &
World Report.
http://www.globalexchange.org/campaigns/fairtrade/stores/fairt
rade.html.

Neil King Jr. (2003) *Bush Officials Draft Broad Plan for Free
Market Economy in Iraq*. Wall Street Journal.

Korten, Dr. David. *When Corporations Rule the World.* San Francisco, CA: Barrett-Koehler Publishers.

New Rules for the Global Economy. AFL-CIO. http://www.aflcio.org/issuespolitics/globaleconomy/newrules.cfm.

Of Debt, Deflation, and Denial. (2002) Economist Magazine. http://www.economist.com/finance/displayStory.cfm?story_id =1382605.

Privatization. Wikipedia, The Free Encyclopedia. http://en.wikipedia.org/wiki/Privatization#Arguments_against_privatization.

Schumer, Charles, Roberts, Paul Craig. (2004) *Second Thoughts on Free Trade.* New York Times.

Smith, Adam. (1991) *The Wealth of Nations.* Prometheus Books.

Conclusion

Wilkins, Roger. (2001) *Jefferson's Pillow.* Beacon Press.

Huffington, Arianna. (2004) *Pigs at the Trough.* New York: Three Rivers Press.

BOOK AVAILABLE THROUGH

Milligan Books, Inc.

THIEVES IN THE TEMPLE $14.95

Order Form

Milligan Books, Inc.

1425 W. Manchester Ave., Suite C, Los Angeles, CA 90047

(323) 750-3592

Name_____ Date _____

Address_____

City_____ State____ Zip Code _____

Day Telephone _____

Evening Telephone_____

Book Title_____

Number of books ordered___ Total ....$ _____

Sales Taxes (CA Add 8.25%) ....$ _____

Shipping & Handling $4.90 for one book ..$ _____

Add $1.00 for each additional book ....$ _____

Total Amount Due....................................$ _____

☐ Check   ☐ Money Order ☐ Other Cards _____

☐ Visa   ☐ MasterCard Expiration Date _____

Credit Card No. _____

Driver License No. _____

Make check payable to Milligan Books, Inc.

_____   _____

Signature   Date

CPSIA information can be obtained at www.ICGtesting.com
Printed in the USA
BVOW041103180911

271529BV00003B/22/A